Hitchcock's Bi-Textuality

SUNY Series in Psychoanalysis and Culture
Henry Sussman, Editor

Hitchcock's Bi-Textuality

Lacan, Feminisms, and Queer Theory

ROBERT SAMUELS

STATE UNIVERSITY OF NEW YORK PRESS

Published by
State University of New York Press, Albany

For information, address State University of New York Press, State University Plaza, Albany, N.Y., 12246

Production by Diane Ganeles
Marketing by Nancy Farrell

Library of Congress Cataloging-in-Publication Data

Samuels, Robert, 1961–
    Hitchcock's bi-textuality : Lacan, feminisms, and queer theory / Robert Samuels.
        p.   cm. — (SUNY series in psychoanalysis and culture)
    Includes index.
    ISBN 0-7914-3609-8 (alk. paper). — ISBN 0-7914-3610-1 (pbk. : alk. paper)
    1. Hitchcock, Alfred, 1899–   —Criticism and interpretation.
I. Title.   II. Series.
PN1998.3.H58S26   1998
791.43'0233'092—dc21   97-1209
                                                        CIP

10 9 8 7 6 5 4 3 2 1

For Jacqueline, with love.

Laura Scott.

Contents

Acknowledgments

I would like to thank Thomas Cohen for first teaching me how to read Hitchcock. I am also indebted to the work of Slavoj Zizek, Judith Butler, Kaja Silverman, and Julia Kristeva. This book would not have been possible without the help of Mark Bracher, Ronald Corthell, and Henry Sussman.

Introduction

The central focus of this book combines an articulation of Jacque Lacan's theory of ethics with a discussion of recent theories of feminine subjectivity and bisexuality. Through a close reading of Hitchcock's films, I will argue that just as Freud posited a fundamental ground of bisexuality for every subject, we can affirm a form of universal bi-textuality that is repressed through different modes of representation yet returns in unconscious aspects of textuality (dreams, word-play, jokes, and symbolism). In order to illustrate this notion of "bi-textuality," I will show how Hitchcock's films are extremely heterogeneous and present multiple forms of sexual identification and desire, although they have most often been read through the reductive lens of male heterosexuality.

Hitchcock's work can be used to articulate Lacan's theory of ethics, which is based on a critical theory of representation. Lacan argues that we negate the Real by representing it and that this act of Symbolic destruction or murder is at the root of all of our unconscious guilt. In Hitchcock's films, we find a clear illustration of this connection between our acts of representation and our killing off of the Real. We shall see that for Hitchcock, the question of murder is always tied to the processes of representation that seek to contain and control diverse forms of unconscious desire.

My contention is that any postmodern theory of ethics must take into account these unconscious bisexual desires and identifications, as well as, the ideological processes that

1

account for repression and societal censorship. Furthermore, Lacan's fundamental claim that we are not in control of language and our sexual representations implies that any attempt to master language and sexuality is always coupled with a projection of lack and loss onto other subjects and objects. A new ethical theory of reading must reverse this process in order to give a voice to repressed sexualities and subjectivities.

One way that current theorists have attempted to resist dominant male-centered modes of discourse is by offering a new form of language under the banner of feminine writing (*écriture féminine*).[1] I will argue in the first two chapters of this book that Hitchcock anticipates this connection between femininity and writing in his two early films *The Lady Vanishes* and *Spellbound*.[2] In the first film, the presence of written letters is directly connected to the return of the lost female who vanishes on the masculine-controlled train. I interpret this "vanishing lady" as a symbol of the way that feminine subjectivity and sexuality are repressed beneath the phallocentric Symbolic order. In *Spellbound*, we witness the masculine anxiety in front of the resisting female subject who represents the loss of the phallic control of language.

In chapter 3, I continue this exploration of the themes of feminine subjectivity, masculine anxiety, and writing by interpreting the film *Rebecca* in light of Judith Butler's book *Bodies That Matter*.[3] Butler's theory allows us to examine the different ways that feminine sexuality and subjectivity are materialized in forms of representation that resist our traditional (heterosexual) notions of logic and desire. In the case of *Rebecca*, the circulation of desire between women serves to undermine the masculine death drive and the cultural attempt to control feminine sexuality and subjectivity.

In chapter 4, I examine Luce Irigaray's claim that feminine writing and desire differentiates itself from traditional models of male-centered discourse through a stress on the fluidity of female bodies and forms of speech.[4] By reading the film *Notorious*, I will show how Hitchcock continuously plays on the difference between masculine forms of enclosure and feminine forms of fluidity by highlighting the feminine disruption of the masculine desire for visual order and control.

The next two films that I analyze, *Vertigo* and *Marnie*, deal explicitly with the process of a masculine attempt at remolding and controlling the feminine form. These films depict how the fluidity of feminine desire and discourse becomes stabilized and fixed in representational structures that are controlled by men. In reading both of these movies, I will explain how the masculine representational death drive attempts to void women of all levels of spontaneity, agency, and control.

The visual control of women by men is a strong theme that runs throughout *Rear Window*. This film has already received much feminist criticism; yet, I would like to argue that most theorists have relied on Laura Mulvey's early article "Visual Pleasure and Narrative Cinema," which in many ways uses Lacan to say the exact opposite of what he was most often arguing.[5] By reversing Mulvey's interpretation, I will articulate how Lacan's notion of the "gaze" offers a valuable tool for resistant forms of feminine representation. For Lacan, the gaze is precisely that part of the visual world that refuses to be controlled or mastered. In its structure, the gaze proves masculine castration and not, as Mulvey argues, the control of the visual field. I believe that Mulvey's reading is an ideological one that does not take into account the true nature of unconscious and bi-textual desire.

This question of ideological interpretations and unconscious forms of textuality and sexuality is a central theme of my reading of *The Birds* and Slavoj Zizek's analysis of this film.[6] In order to stress the resistant nature of bi-textual desire and the gaze, I examine the function of the "maternal super-ego" in Zizek's and Hitchcock's work and how the presence of this agency is tied to an ideology that serves to "block" the awareness of unconscious desire and discourse.[7]

In the final chapter of this book, I argue that *Psycho* represents a return of all of Hitchcock's, and our own culture's, most repressed feelings and images concerning feminine sexuality, bi-textuality, and desire. At the same time, *Psycho*, also, deals with the taking over of the masculine body by a female voice and the radical subjective splitting that this process requires.

The Presentation and Repression
of Bisexual Textuality

From a certain angle, the ending of *Psycho* presents a reversal of one of the central themes of Hitchcock's work, which is the control of the female body by a masculine voice and author.[8] To counter this heterosexual division of labor between the feminine image and the masculine voice, I will argue throughout this book that Hitchcock's subjects are inherently bisexual and that the director's own identifications represent multiple forms of desire and identification.[9] I, therefore, propose to combine my reading of the theme of feminine subjectivity with an analysis of the role of bisexual textuality or "bi-textuality." These two readings come together because of the way that Hitchcock himself "over-identifies" with his feminine characters.

In chapter 1, I provide a reading of *The Lady Vanishes* that shows how the director clearly associates himself with the female subject, Iris, who is looking for the lost feminine figure on the masculine train. Likewise, in chapter 2, I argue that in *Spellbound*, the horror that the male subject shows in his encounter with feminine sexuality represents a displaced horror that he feels about his own sexuality and his presence in the world. In this structure, the feminine object is tied to the projection of a masculine recognition of loss and lack within language.[10]

The theme of bisexual subjectivity comes to the foreground in chapter 3 where I analyze *Rebecca* and Hitchcock's presentation of the circulation of feminine desire between women in an open manner. The unnamed female subject of the film is constantly placed in the position of either accepting or denying her identification as the second Mrs. de Winter as well as her role in the economy of feminine desire.[11] The fact that this lesbian homosocial structure of the film has most often been ignored can be attributed to the way that most critics, even feminist theorists, have insisted on reading all texts within an essentially male heterosexual paradigm. One of the reasons for the persistence of this "narrow" way of reading is that a more open analysis of sexuality and textuality often results in a destabilization of the field of representation.

In *Notorious*, it is precisely the visual realm of representation that is called into question and subverted by the presence of a flowing feminine desire that refuses to be contained within certain masculine-controlled structures of discourse. Whereas we can easily identify Hitchcock with the masculine characters in the film that attempt to contain and control this feminine fluidity, I argue in my fourth chapter that we can also associate the director to the presence of the feminine flow and the disruption of the visual field.

In chapter 5, I show that *Vertigo* continues this theme of Hitchcock's bisexual identifications by identifying the spying male protagonist with the lost female object he desires to re-find and re-see. In a crucial dream sequence, Hitchcock has the melancholic male subject fall in the exact manner that the lost female subject has previously fallen, and in this sense the death of the female object is equated with the loss of the male subject himself.

The theme of masculine loss and lack returns in chapter 6, where I argue that in *Marnie* the female subject not only continuously steals money from men, but also steals the grounding of their sexual identity. Furthermore, Marnie's sexuality is itself posed as a question mark that moves between self-abjection and an affirmation of a repressed bisexual desire. This notion of an unacknowledged homosexual and bisexual desire is also a central aspect of my reading of *Rear Window* (chapter 7). By rethinking both the notions of the gaze and the fetish, I insist that what the voyeur really wants to see is the presentation of a bisexual object. However, this bisexual dimension is continuously overlooked in the film for certain ideological reasons that I analyze in chapter 8 through my reading of *The Birds* in conjunction with Slavoj Zizek's theory of the ideological fantasy.

The final chapter of this book explores the theme of bisexuality as it is presented in *Psycho*—a threat that brings on the possibility of psychosis. By placing the bisexual subject in a psychotic structure, Hitchcock allows us to see why we have such a horror of our own Real unconscious desires. Bisexuality and bi-textuality serve to undermine all of our stable illusions of identity and our ability to control language as well as the general field of representation. Throughout this book, I will argue that any theory of ethics must be centered on both the presence and repression of unconscious bi-textuality.

Ethics and Representation

Central to Lacan's theory of ethics is the idea that the death drive represents the way that humans replace Real things with Symbolic representations.[12] Yet, Lacan also insists that this process of replacement is resisted by the subject of the unconscious who feels guilty about the destruction of the natural realm. The primordial feeling of guilt of every subject, which Martin Heidegger explores at the end of *Being and Time*, is not a guilt due to a particular action or intention; rather, it is a fundamental realization of the relation between the Real and the Symbolic. This ethical argument is primarily outlined in Lacan's seminar entitled *The Ethics of Psychoanalysis*.[13] I believe that this text has been consistently misread and that Lacan's new theory of ethics is founded on one of the oldest myths of the Judeo-Christian tradition—the story of the Garden of Eden.[14]

Lacan's seminar on ethics is centered on the dialectical relation between what he calls the "realm of the Thing" (*das Ding*) and the "realm of language" (43–70). For Lacan, language is responsible for the negation or murder of the original natural Thing (63, 68, 70, 239, 295). As in Hegel's theory, because we have language and different forms of Symbolic representation, we are estranged or alienated from the Real of nature. These theories repeat the myth of the Garden of Eden where Adam and Eve are forced out of their natural state because they are punished for eating from the tree of knowledge.[15] This original myth is clearly structured by the binary opposition between life and knowledge, just as Lacan's theory is structured by the opposition between the Thing and language and, later on in his work, between life and meaning.[16]

Furthermore, in order to connect his theory of linguistic alienation to Freud's theory of the Oedipus Complex, Lacan argues that the original Thing for every subject is the mother and that the mother is forbidden by the law of the father or what is otherwise known as the incest taboo (67–68). "What we find in the incest law is located as such at the level of the unconscious in relation to *das Ding*, the Thing" (68). In this theory, the Real mother-Thing is negated or transcended by the Symbolic law of the father that then forces the desire for the mother into the subject's unconscious.

At the heart of Lacan's seminar on ethics is this attempt to equate the Oedipus Complex with the general structure of language. Just as language continues to circle the absent referent or Real, the subject that passes through the Oedipus Complex continues to desire the lost mother. In this sense, the lost referent of language is equivalent to the lost object of desire. Furthermore, Lacan insists that since Freud's reality principle is dependent on the subject's ability to refind a lost object, every attempt at re-presenting something must include the structure of desire: "The world of our experience, the Freudian world, assumes that it is this object, *das Ding*, as the absolute Other of the subject, that one is supposed to find again. It is to be found at the most as something missed" (52). Following Freud, Lacan argues that one can never refind the original thing that one is looking for; rather, one can only find the absence of the Thing. Thus, Lacan is not only saying here that "absence makes the heart grow fonder," but he also is affirming that the cause of every subject's desire is an object that presents the original loss of the Thing (*das Ding*).

Since every ethical theory is tied to the possibility of discourse, law, representation, and language, Lacan argues that if one wants to talk about ethics in general, one has to take into account the way that these different Symbolic processes function. In fact, he goes as far as saying that the taboo against incest provides for the distance between the subject and the Real that makes the very existence of speech and morality possible (69).

Moreover, Lacan takes Freud's theories of the death drive, the reality principle, and the Oedipus Complex and reads them on a Symbolic and mythical level. He affirms that when Freud turns to his theory of the death drive, what he really is doing is attempting to account for the power of language to efface the forces of life. In other words, the death drive is a myth that accounts for the way that subjects are civilized and transformed into linguistic beings. One of the problems with this process of symbolization is that like in the example of Adam, there is always a part of the Real that cannot be consumed by language.

In Adam's case, there is a residue of the apple that sticks in his throat in the form of what we call the "Adam's apple." Lacan adds in *The Four Fundamental Concepts of Psychoanalysis*, that the object (*a*) cannot be swallowed in the throat of the Symbolic (270). In this sense, the object (*a*) or the Adam's apple is a reminder or a remainder of the Real that has resisted being submitted to the death drive and the process of Symbolic civilization. It is this object that then becomes the cause of unconscious desire.

A central element of Lacan's theory of ethics is his belief that at the foundation of all of our guilt is our awareness of the way that we destroy the Real by Symbolizing it. Thus, our original sin is repeated every time that we speak or articulate something in a Symbolic form. Lacan says this in a cryptic way, when he states in *The Ethics of Psychoanalysis* that the death drive is "an obscure transgression which calls for punishment" (2). I will attempt to show in several of Hitchcock's films the way that this allegory of linguistic transgression, punishment, and guilt is presented. In other words, Hitchcock's films are only superficially murder mysteries and spy thrillers. More profoundly they are meditations on the ethics of representation.[17] We will find that this ethical dimension in Hitchcock's work is often presented through the "projection" of different unconscious formations such as dreams, wordplays, slips, faulty actions, and jokes. For it is only through the unconscious that the subject's true bi-textual desire is allowed to emerge beyond the resistance of his or her ego.

As in most classical narratives, it is often a woman who plays the role of the lost object that causes a man to desire in Hitchcock's films. Since desire is always a desire for something that one doesn't have, the key to the feminine object will be the presentation of a form of absence. We must remember that, for Freud, desire is always unconscious and that the subject of the unconscious continually wishes to return to his or her first objects that have now been lost. However, if these initial objects are lost because of the structure of language, the subject can only hope to refind its desire outside of the Symbolic order. In other words, the feminine object is forced to represent a presence that is beyond language and other forms of Symbolic representation.[18] With Hitchcock's films, we will be able to trace what I will call here the "vanishing of the female subject" and its reappearance in the form of the unrepresentable object.

For Lacan, the subject of the unconscious is not only aware of the way that language replaces the Real, but also the subject resists this process. In his eleventh seminar, Lacan refers to the subject as a "hole" (22), a "gap" (21,29) or a "split" (25,31) in the structure of language and because this subject cannot find a place in the Symbolic realm of the Other, it is represented by being barred.[19] Lacan writes the symbol of the subject as "$", in order to stress the way that the subject is "subjected" to the transcendent Symbolic order.

I will insist that in Hitchcock's work, we find a representation of this theory of the barred subject on several different levels. First of all, the subject of Hitchcock's films are often misidentified—they either take on other people's identities or they are mistaken for someone else. This fluidity between self and identity is caused by the way that the Real subject of the unconscious resists all forms of Symbolization and is thus essentially a subject without a name. In Lacan's terms, the subject lacks a signifier of identification and thus Symbols of identification must always come from the place of the social Other.

Second, Hitchcock often shows his subjects with a shadow running across their bodies as if he is representing the way that they are barred by the Symbolic order. The accused man is one whose death or imprisonment has been foreshadowed. For Lacan, the barred subject is barred because he or she has been subjected to the Symbolic order of language that goes beyond the intentionality of the ego.

Linked to this profound awareness of the barred subject of language is Lacan's notion that if consciousness is always consciousness of another object, image or person, the ego is

itself pure nothingness.[20] This argument results in two central effects: (1) the subject is narcissistically invested in all of
its external representations; and (2) the subject represses
any awareness of its own nothingness or its own lack of representation. Furthermore, in order for the ego to avoid the
encounter with its own lack, it must project it into the place
of the Other and then use this nothingness, or what Lacan
calls the "object" (*a*), as a cause of its own desire or anxiety.

In our current civilization and social structure, this
dialectic between the Imaginary state of consciousness and
the projected object of nothingness is most often played out
in gendered and racial terms.[21] Thus, men project onto
women their own nothingness and then claim that the
woman is castrated or missing the phallus.[22] The next step in
this process is the eroticization of the female body around
this central lack. Women in this way become the substitute
for the unsymbolizable Real, which subjects then seek out in
their unconscious desire. The option for female subjects is
then to either play their part as the unrepresentable object
that causes desire or to identify with the male in their desire
for the female object that can be located either in themselves
(narcissism) or in another woman (lesbianism). What most
radical readings of gender politics often fail to take into
account is this structure of the projection of nothingness.
Likewise, in the study of racial prejudice, what is often
ignored is the way that the Other becomes reduced to being
this object of pure nothingness, which in this case becomes
not a source of eroticization, but rather a cause of anxiety.

The Ethics of the Real

In this book, I will argue that Lacan's ethical theory is
centered on the way that language both bars and produces
subjects. At the same time, I will insist on the way that
Lacan seeks to constitute an ethics of the Real, which he
opposes to any type of ideal morality:

> Well, as odd as it may seem to that superficial opinion
> that assumes any inquiry into ethics must concern the

field of the ideal, if not the unreal, I, on the contrary will precede from the other direction by going more deeply into the notion of the real. Insofar as Freud's position constitutes progress here, the question of ethics is to be articulated from the point of view of the location of man's relation to the real. (11)

We may question here the gendered position of the relation to the Real, however, I believe that Lacan's attempt to dissociate ethics from any type of ideal morality opens up the possibility for the recognition of diverse forms of desire, sexuality, and subjectivity.

An ethics of the Real can only be an ethics based on unconscious bisexual and multi-textual desire. For it is only on the level of our heterogeneous desire that we acknowledge the Real that we continue to negate and avoid. Hitchcock's films offer us an opportunity to witness this effacement and return of unconscious desire and yet we can only witness what we are willing to read. An ethics of reading is thus a necessary component to our theory of bi-textuality.

1

The Lady Vanishes, but the Letter Remains:
Kristeva and the Maternal Real(m)

Hitchcock's early film, *The Lady Vanishes* has received much analysis from a feminist perspective. On one level, it can be read as an allegory of the losing and the regaining of the lost maternal object in the figure of Miss Froy.[1] From another perspective, it has been viewed as the attempt to express the feminine desire of Iris, the woman who is about to be married but becomes "derailed" once she encounters the mystery of Miss Froy's disappearance and the presence of her helper and future lover, Gilbert.[2] I would like to argue that before one enters into the different ideological interpretations of this film, one must first examine what can be called the "materiality" of the text.[3]

The Hotel of Babel

The story begins with a view of mountains and then the panning camera enters into a hotel. At first there is silence and then a cacophony of voices in different foreign languages emerges. The hotel takes on the air of being a veritable Tower of Babel. It is as if Hitchcock was saying to us: "See what happens when you add voice to film? Wasn't it better when things were just silent and the language of film was produced through the pure medium of the image—A medium that was much more universal and did not have to suffer from the particularity of different languages?" Is Hitchcock telling us that even though language is full of sound and fury, it still signifies nothing?

I will argue that not only does the opening of the film comment on the transition between silent film and talking films, but it also sets up a binary opposition between masculine-controlled speech and a feminine form of writing. I hope to show how the "phallocentric" control of speech in the film (and in Hitchcock's work in general) is constantly subverted by another form of language that centers around the insistence of letters, blocked images, and writing.[4]

By starting off with a scene of silent images, Hitchcock is able to illustrate the transition from the pre-Oedipal Imaginary order to the post-Oedipal Symbolic order. In Lacan's theory, this movement of transition from the Imaginary to the Symbolic is structured by what he calls the "paternal metaphor."[5] This rhetorical trope accounts for the dominance of the masculine Name-of-the-Father over the maternal realm of Imaginary desire. To be a subject of language and law, for Lacan, means that one has given up one's Imaginary dual relation with one's (m)other or ideal and has identified with the Symbolic Other through the internalization of the super-ego.

In the structure of the paternal metaphor, one's desire to return to the mother is repressed into the realm of the unconscious by the binding power of the law against incest. Every act of speech and symbolization, then, serves to reenact this separation between the Real subject and the Imaginary mother-figure. In this sense, language is itself Oedipal and patriarchal, because in our culture men are most often associated with the law and women with images.

Lacan in part bases the connection between the paternal function and the Symbolic signifier on the fact that it is always a question who the biological father of a child is, while it is always clear who the Real mother is. "The attribution of the procreation to the father can only be the effect of a pure signifier, of a recognition, not of a real father, but of what religion has taught us to refer to the Name-of-the-Father" (199). In *The Lady Vanishes*, this connection between language and paternity is constantly stressed, as well as put into question.

In one of the first scenes of the film, Iris is talking to her friends about her upcoming marriage and she states that: "I shall take the veil . . . and change my name to Mrs. Charles Fotheringale . . . I've no regrets." By being submitted to the veil of marriage, Iris, thus, desires to take on the name of Fotheringale, a last name that sounds very close to father. In response to her vow to get married, one of her friends asks her: "Couldn't you get him to change his name instead?" This question shows an awareness of the way that a female's identity can vanish beneath the name of her husband. To paraphrase Hegel, we can say that the Name is the death of "The Lady" because the female subject vanishes beneath the Name-of-the-Father and her presence now becomes veiled.

This movement of repressing the female subject beneath the father's name, anticipates the disappearance of the maternal figure, Miss Froy, on the train. What I would like to examine later is the connection between these two disappearances, but for now I will turn to a scene of feminine writing that counters the dominance of the paternal metaphor.

A Scene of Feminine Writing

Miss Froy takes Iris to the dining car of the train that they are on. Since they have not yet been formally introduced, Miss Froy begins to say her name but the train whistle blows and her voice is drowned out. Iris asks her if she said her name was "Freud." She replies, "No Froy, it rhymes with Joy." Here we find a double reference to the founder of psychoanalysis and the rhyming power of language.

By saying that her name rhymes with joy, Miss Froy is trying to communicate to her listener, not on a level of signification nor meaning, but rather on the level of sound and identity. However, this attempt to communicate through speech ultimately fails so Miss Froy writes her name on the window by tracing the letters "F-R-O-Y." If we see the window as the screen or even as the lens of the camera, we could insist that Hitchcock is attempting to show his preference for film writing over film speech.

Miss Froy's resistance to the paternal metaphor is signaled by the way that she attempts to play on the metonymic aspect of language and not on its metaphoric side.[6] In his "Agency of the Letter in the Unconscious," Lacan distinguishes metaphor from metonymy by arguing that metonymy is concerned with the connection and displacement between signifiers, while metaphor works by replacing one signifier with another signifier and thus inducing an effect of signification (164). In this theory, metaphor points towards the creation of meaning, while, metonymy is determined by the movement of desire and the production of new word associations.

We can illustrate this difference between metaphor and metonymy by looking at the difference between the productions of Iris's name and Miss Froy's name. In Iris' case, she has decided to let her husband's name substitute for her own name. The manifest signification of this process is that society now recognizes her to be her husband's wife. I would add that the repressed signification of this process is that she has now lost her own identity by being subjected to the name of the Other.

In opposition to this metaphorical structure, the unmarried Miss Froy plays on the letteral level of language. She first highlights the aural aspect of language by pointing out the rhyme between Froy and joy and then she accentuates the visual part of language by writing her name on the window. In both instances, she is not producing a new meaning; rather, she is attempting to materialize through sound and vision, the immaterial signifier.

This attempt to give a material foundation to language, represents one of the central elements of Lacan's return to Freud. In the "Agency of the Letter," Lacan states that, "by 'letter' I designate that material support that concrete discourse borrows from language" (147). Lacan wants to turn to this materiality of language, in part, to show how many of Freud's discoveries about the unconscious are founded on a careful attentiveness to the play of letters and are not based on a concern for meaning.

An example of this insistence of the metonymic letter in the unconscious can be found in Freud's discussion of his dream of the botanical monograph. In his interpretation of this unconscious production, Freud argues that: "'Botanical' was related to the figure of Professor Gartner, the blooming looks of his wife, to my patient Flora, and to the lady of whom I had told the story of the forgotten flowers."[7] The movement of these associations follows the insistence of the letter in the unconscious. The connection between botanical, Gartner, blooming, Flora, and Flower has nothing to do with any actual or lived connection but is motivated by the play of the signifier.

From the concept botanical to the name Gartner, the association is based on the literal derivation of the proper name—Professor Gartner is only a gardener in name and not in life. Likewise, the pregnant wife is only related to the Gardner in the sense that she is blooming, after a seed has been placed in her. Here, the connection is based on a "litaralized" metaphor. The next association to his patient Flora is also only motivated by the insistence of the letters in her name that connects her to the general theme of flowers. This example shows how the unconscious connection between different dream associations is determined by the metonymical movement between signifiers and letters.

According to Julia Kristeva, the unconscious is inherently revolutionary and poetic because it plays on this level of the letter and not on the level of meaning and social restraint:

> Murder, death, and unchanging society represent precisely the inability to hear and understand the signifier as such—as ciphering, as rhythm, as a presence that precedes the signification of object and emotion. The poet is put to death because he wants to turn rhythm into a dominant element; because he wants to make language perceive what it doesn't want to say, provide it with matter independently of the sign, and free it from denotation.[8]

This description of the threat of the poetic can be applied equally to Freud and to Miss Froy. We must not forget that this female spy on the train is kidnapped and threatened with death, because she sings a certain song that has a secret code ciphered into it. Thus, her song highlights the dimensions of rhythm, ciphering, and presence that Kristeva insists defines poetry and the unconscious resistance to the dominant social order of the paternal metaphor.

A feminine way of speaking and writing for Kristeva involves, in part, a return to the maternal realm of rhythm, sound, and materiality. "The unsettled and questionable subject of poetic language . . . maintains itself at the cost of reactivating this repressed instinctual, maternal element" (136). What defines this maternal element for Kristeva is a lack of identity, and a dominance of instincts, rhythm, and matter.

In Hitchcock's film, we find a remarkable illustration of these maternal elements when we see, superimposed, the rhythmic movement of the train wheels with the multiplication of the images of Iris's friends. The rhythm of the train puts Iris to sleep and allows for her to "regress" back to the maternal realm of confused images and sounds.[9] In this sense, her search for the Lady who has vanished can be read as representing her desire to return to a state that is positioned as being before the imposition of social order and law.

If, in order to become a subject of language, one has to accept the paternal metaphor and distance oneself from the realm of the mother, poetic language and feminine writing represent a reversal of this process. Furthermore, in Lacan's notion of the ethical unconscious, it is only through the material (and we can add maternal) insistence of the letter that the subject maintains a relation with the Real. Hitchcock in his work continuously shows that the Real evidence or traces that are left behind in a crime are letters and written signs because words vanish in thin air, but letters tend to remain.

This insistence of the letter is borne out when Iris begins to look for proof of Miss Froy's existence. Every one on the train says that they never saw her. In fact, they are all lying because they have something to hide. In this way, Hitchcock links spoken language to deception, and it is only by following the traces of letters and writing that Iris will be able to discover the truth about the Lady.

The first form of proof that Iris collects of the Lady's existence is the letters that Miss Froy has traced on the window. My hypothesis is that this scene allegorizes the way that speech serves to efface women and that it is only through a form of feminine writing that their presence is allowed to reemerge. In other words, we can read Iris's pursuit of the lost Lady as her search for a form of feminine existence that is continuously denied by the males on the train.

The second "material evidence" that Iris finds is the teabag box label that has been discarded and has ended up stuck against a window of the train. Tea, whose very name is a homonym for the letter *T*, is represented by the repetition of the letter *H*, which is found in the brand name "Harriman's Herbal Tea." Furthermore, Iris's last name is Henderson and throughout the film we see her wearing and holding things with her initials *I H* clearly displayed. One could read this insistence of her initials as an indication of Hitchcock himself; as if he is saying that "I am H." We shall see how this insistence of letters in the names of Hitchcock's character's can never be ignored.

In fact, the name "Iris" can be read as a double reference to the *I* and the "eye." She is the one who has seen the Lady and who is looking for the proof of her absence. We, as the audience, are placed in her position; we are the eye that is looking for the presence of the lost object, just as Hitchcock is trying to look for the Real object that has been effaced through the process of representation. On the level of speech, every one denies the Lady's existence, but on the level of writing, her presence is retained. Once again, we find here the association of speech, deception, death, and disappearance on the one hand, and presence, truth, and writing on the other.

So far I have related the vanishing of the Lady to the "fading" of the female subject below the patriarchic structure that drowns out the female voice. In this sense, the Lady vanishes because she has no place in the male-directed discourse of film representation, just as the subject vanishes beneath the power of language and the desire of the Other. Early in the film, Hitchcock illustrates this structure by placing Gilbert's room right above Iris's; Gilbert is literally the signifier that stands above her and drowns out her voice.

When Miss Froy and Iris first meet, they are in the hallway of the hotel and they both are complaining about the noise that is coming from above them. Iris decides to call Boris, the head of the hotel, to get him to stop the musical noise. When Boris enters Gilbert's room, he sees three servants doing a folk dance under Gilbert's instructions. Each time Gilbert stops playing his phallic clarinet, he has the servants stop in their place, and he writes down their positions. This scene, in part, shows how masculine discourse serves to regulate the movements of the body.

When Boris asks Gilbert to stop the noise, Gilbert's reaction is very telling. He exclaims, "You dare call it noise. The ancient music which your present ancestors celebrated every wedding for countless generations. The dance they danced when your father married your mother." Here, Gilbert's music and discourse is directly tied to the social and historical realm of the Name-of-the-Father.

In opposition to Miss Froy's free-floating song, Gilbert's music is regimented and highly structured. This distinction between the paternal and the maternal orders of music becomes most evident at the end of the film, when Miss Froy has entrusted Gilbert with the mission of remembering her secret song for her. During the last part of the film, Gilbert is constantly humming this song, so he won't forget it, but as he enters the lobby of the foreign office, he realizes that he can no longer remember it. Then he starts to hum a song but he realizes that it is the Wedding March. The song of marriage and social union, thus, serves to repress and efface the tune of a secret maternal code.

Luckily for the cause of world peace, Miss Froy has survived and the final scene shows her playing the coded song on a piano. Upon seeing Miss Froy, Gilbert's final line in the film is "I'll be hanged!" Couldn't this be an indication of the threat that is posed by the resurfacing of the maternal realm of the coded song? Gilbert feels that he will lose his head because he can no longer control the material and instinctual side of language.

This forgetting of Miss Froy's song and presence is doubled in the film by Gilbert's constant references to his father and his refusal to acknowledge his mother's role in his own creation. At one point in the film, Gilbert blurts out, "You know, it's remarkable how many great men begin with their fathers." Here the paternal claim for creation is so strong that it completely removes the mother from the act of conception. Kristeva has provided an explanation for this masculine desire to repress the creative role played by the mother: "Fear of the archaic mother turns out to be essentially fear of her generative power. It is this power, a dreaded one, that patrilineal filiation has the burden of subduing."[10] Gilbert's constant references to his father can therefore be related to his attempt to reinforce his paternal metaphor by denying the creative and productive power of his mother.

Miss Froy's return at the end of the film, while it can be seen as a potential threat to Gilbert's paternal order, is maintained and controlled by being placed in the political realm of the Foreign Office. After all, her coded song was written and determined by the men at the British Governmental office. The production of her unconscious discourse is, in this sense, predetermined by a masculine mode of language.

We can also interpret the Foreign Office itself as the locus of the social Other that attempts to control and regulate all of the foreign elements that threaten to undermine the stability of the state. The dialectic between social control and the threat of a foreign destabilizing influence dramatizes, on a social level, the linguistic battle which determines Hitchcock's text. It is also this very dialectic that structures the "The Ethics of Linguistics" for Kristeva:

> Ethics used to be a coercive, customary manner of ensuring the cohesiveness of a particular group through the repetition of a code. . . . Now however, the issue of ethics crops up wherever a code (mores, social contract) must be shattered in order to give way to a free play of negativity, need, desire, pleasure, and jouissance."[11]

Need, desire, pleasure, and jouissance are the foreign elements that serve to threaten any fixed paternal code of order and social regulation. Like Lacan, Kristeva believes that any ethical theory must take these "poetic" elements into account.

In Hitchcock's work we find a careful attention to the way that language is split between these two processes of the paternal metaphor and the maternal metonymy. Like Miss Froy's secret song, Hitchcock uses names in his films in order to point to these two opposing levels of language. The wordplay of father and Fotheringale, as well as Froy and Freud, and Iris with iris, point to an unconscious insistence of the letter inscribed within the dominant discourse and name of the Other. In other words, there is another discourse that has been repressed and is attempting to make itself heard within the central discourse; just as there is an "unconscious text" that at times emerges within the conscious text and plot of the film.

What makes Hitchcock's work so doubly impressive is that he is able to play on both of these levels of language at the same time. Through his use of the paternal metaphor, he makes his films into consumable products by clearly pointing to the paternal control of feminine desire. His constant need to end his films with the resolution of a mystery and the promise of a marriage shows the dominance of a conservative paternal ideology. Yet, at the same time, through his constant meditation on the processes of representation, he allows for a more poetic and feminine form of discourse to emerge. In a similar sense, Freud's careful analysis of the inner workings of Victorian society allowed him to explore both the conservative side of paternal order and also the more radical aspects of language and sexuality. I would argue that any feminist-inspired theory of ethics must be able to articulate and play off of these two combatting linguistic and social forces.

Barring Sexuality

Not only are there multiple forms of textuality that are inherent to Hitchcock's film, but we also find multiple forms of sexuality that are repressed, yet continue to return. In the first scene of the film, we meet two British gentlemen who must share a room and a single bed. Later on we find these same two men in bed together with their pants off. This can be certainly read as a not-so veiled reference to homosexuality. After all there are several references to something "queer" going on in the hotel and on the train.

In another room, we find three women who are undressing and discussing the evils of marriage together. This room also relates to the different forms of sexuality that are permitted behind closed doors but not in the open. In this sense, the hotel that is found in the opening scenes of the film is not only a tower of linguistic Babel and diversity but also of sexual multiplicity and deviation. Once everyone moves from the free-play of the hotel to the enclosed structure of the train, everyone's sexuality is forced back into the closet.

One of the couples that we find in a train compartment is a man and a woman who are both having affairs. When the woman threatens to bring their relation out into the public, the male warns her that he is trying to become a judge and that "the law like Caesar's wife must be beyond suspicion." In other words, on the level of the law of the signifier, there can be no illicit sexuality.

However, we know from Hitchcock's films that no one is beyond suspicion—anyone can be accused of a crime and everyone does commit some crime or other, either in an act or through desire, and therefore everyone is guilty. Yet Hollywood and the American Puritan ethic wishes to deny our acts of transgression, so all must go on behind closed doors. In this sense, behind every door is the subject's unconscious desire. This metaphor is in fact not foreign to Freud, who often argued that the unconscious is like a room that is guarded by a censor.

Returning to the early scene of the two men in the hotel room, which is likened to a closet, we find in the middle of the room a large support beam that cuts across the camera's frame and against which one man continuously bumps his head. I would like to read this black line as the materialization of the social censor and the sign of the barred or repressed subject. Something can't be shown in the scene because the bar is in the way. It is not only therefore the Lady that vanishes in the film, but also different forms of sexuality that are blocked from view.

The black bar is a common symbol in Hitchcock's work and is most often presented in the form of a pillar or a shadow that runs across the body of a character.[12] In the case of the two men who stay in the same room together, we can read the pillar that cuts across the scene as the social barring of homosexuality. We also see in many of Hitchcock's camera angles, some form that is blocking part of the scene. For example, in the scene that follows the two men in the hotel room, Hitchcock directs the camera in such a way that the stairway blocks its view. In fact, part of virtually every scene is eclipsed by some bar or pillar or staircase. It is as if Hitchcock is showing us the proof of the limits of representation in order to open up a nonrepresentational space.

By nonrepresentational space, I am referring to the idea that certain forms of art do not signify through meaning, but rather through form and tone. For instance, Patrice Petro, in her reading of this same movie, draws on Kristeva's work in order to argue that desire is set in motion in the film through the repetition of a song that is nonrepresentational because it foregrounds rhythm, affect, and movement and not the represented plot.[13] In other words, there is something in the scene that cannot be seen nor understood, yet its presence is still felt. I would argue that this unseen presence is the very limit of the field of representation that opens up the space for the emergence of bi-textuality and the return of the vanished Lady.

One can affirm that the presence of feminine desire and existence can only be maintained on this border between the represented and the unrepresented. In a Symbolic world that is dominated by masculine values and definitions, Iris plays the role of the female who refuses to give up her initial relation with the maternal order. All of the men on the train continuously attempt to get her to stop her search for her lost object, Miss Froy, but she resists. Dr. Hartz tells her that her memory of the Lady is only "a vivid subjective image" and that a concussion "may have curious effects upon an imaginative person." He thus tries to convince her that she is lost in the Imaginary and that she should pull herself back into reality.

However, I would like to counter Dr. Hartz and insist that Iris's refusal to accept Miss Froy's absence represents an attempt to resist the deadening effects of language that are based on the primal separation from the mother and the Imaginary order.[14] As Freud argues in *Beyond the Pleasure Principle*, in order for a subject to become a subject of culture and language, he or she must first overcome his or her attachment to the mother and his or her instinctual needs.[15] Lacan adds to this theory in his seminar *The Ethics of Psychoanalysis* that the word is the death of the Thing and that the primal Thing for every subject is the Mother (67).

In an essay appropriately entitled for our purposes, "The Lady Vanishes: Sophie Freud and Beyond the Pleasure Principle," Elisabeth Bronfen argues that Freud's development of his theory of the death drive in *Beyond the Pleasure Principle* is tied to the death of his daughter Sophie.[16] As is well known, in this text, Freud observes Sophie's son playing with a cotton-reel, whose disappearance and reappearance represents the child's attempt to transcend the Real comings and goings of his mother by mastering her absence on a Symbolic level of play. Thus, instead of dealing with the absence and presence of his mother, the child first plays with the absence and presence of his toy and finally with the German words for absence (fort—gone) and presence (*da*—there). Bronfen summarizes the effect of this game in the following passage:

> In the narratives that use this fort-da game as privileged example for the child's acquisition of language, it functions as an allegory for the symbolic mastery of sensations and commentators of this narrative posit that the origin of language and subjectivity is based on loss, on the figurative "murder" of the body, the soma, the thing, the real; representation is grounded on absence of the referred-to object. (983)

What is therefore lost in the gaining of language is an unmediated access to "sensations," "the body," "the soma," "the thing," "the rea,l" and "the referred-to object." In Freud's, Lacan's, and Kristeva's theories all of these lost elements of the Real and of the body are tied to the separation that society places between the mother and the infant.

Iris's refusal to forget about Miss Froy's existence, then, represents a desire to return to the Real and to a state of nonseparation. It will be my argument that this resistance to the Symbolic death drive is representative of Hitchcock's general relation to language and the field of representation. As a film director, he is placed in the phallic role of dictating the rules and regulations of a certain form of representation, yet his obsession with the feminine form and the realm of material images places him in a position that is analogous to the resisting feminine object.

The Ethical Return to the Real

Hitchcock's ethical unconscious is therefore determined by his own desire to return to an initial state of pure sound and vision, before language and social hierarchy are placed in their dominant positions. Yet, simultaneously, he shows a certain horror of the unsymbolized Real and the feminine and homosexual figures that are forced into representing this limit to language and the knowable. Like all subjects of the unconscious, he desires to return to a state of pure sexual excitement, what Lacan calls "jouissance," however, he still fears being lost in this primitive state of the undifferentiated Real.

The Lady Vanishes, in this sense, allegorizes the way that women are used in films to manifest both the foundations and limits of all forms of representation. As an object of exchange, the Lady circulates a coded message, but as an object of desire, she makes present an absence that causes one to desire to know. Thus, the representation of women in film is used to support the paternal metaphor by circulating the effects of power of the masculine-controlled signifier, while at the same time their presence continuously threatens discourse by presenting the maternal metonymy of the letteral insistence of the Real. The combination of these two opposing modes of discourse creates a bi-textual form of sexuality and representation. Furthermore, the insistence of the materiality of the immaterial signifier serves to combine together the visual and aural aspects of language in a form of unconscious textuality that resists the deadening effects of the Symbolic death drive.

2

The Fear of Women and Writing in *Spellbound*:
Kaja Silverman and the Question of Castration

Hitchcock's *Spellbound* can be read as a reaction to the theme of feminine writing that I have analyzed in *The Lady Vanishes*. For I will show how the main male character in this film, John Ballantine, displays a certain horror for both the presence of feminine sexuality and the emergence of writing. These two causes of his anxiety will be related together through the structure of repetition that runs throughout the film. In order to examine these themes, I will turn to Kaja Silverman's work on the questions of castration, fetishism, film theory, and marginalized masculine subjectivity.[1]

Two Theories of Castration

In her book *The Acoustic Mirror*, Silverman argues that Lacan posits a form of linguistic castration and Symbolic murder that predates the discovery of sexual difference. "With Lacan . . . there is a castration which precedes the recognition of anatomical difference—a castration to which all cultural subjects must submit, since it coincides with separation from the world of objects, and the entry into language" (1). The first murder of the Thing thus represents the original separation between the Real world of things and the Symbolic world of language and not primarily the separation between the mother and the child, nor the separation between the sexes.

This initial form of castration is then only recast in terms of sexual differences after-the-fact through its Symbolic repetition. To use one of Lacan's theories of discourse, we can say that the first signifier (the master signifier—S1) serves to separate the subject from the Real, by alienating him or her in the Symbolic, while the second signifier or signifying chain (S2) reinterprets this initial separation through the knowledge of sexual difference.[2] I will write this structure out by using Lacan's discourse of the master:

$$\frac{S1}{\$}\text{-------->}S2$$

The left side of the diagram points to the subject's alienation in language, while the right side indicates the way that this alienation is reinterpreted through the binary code of sexual difference.

As in the case of the repetition-compulsion, the desire to repeat the scene of castration is dependent on a desire to master the initial anxiety of a trauma through its Symbolic reproduction. Silverman adds that this structure of repetition in film takes on the formation of a fetish: "It projects male lack onto female characters in the guise of anatomical deficiency and discourse inadequacy" (1). In other words, because men do not want to face the possibility that they are not in control of language and that they are in fact castrated by the Symbolic order, they project onto their Other a sense of loss and lack. We can also hypothesize along these lines that if women are often equated with the unsymbolizable Real, they are placed in this position in order for men to ward off their own feelings of linguistic alienation.

By separating the initial form of castration from the secondary form of sexual difference, we are able to respond to a number of criticisms that have often been leveled against Freud and Lacan. Critics of psychoanalysis have rightly questioned whether the structures of castration and the Oedipus Complex are historically and culturally derived and not the fixed and universal structures that psychoanalysis makes us think that they are?[3] In fact, I would argue that the first part of the master discourse defines the universal and synchronic imposition of the signifier on the subject for all speaking beings, while the signifying chain (S2) represents the various ways that this imposition has been translated and reinterpreted by the Other.

The master discourse, in this sense, refers to the way that the master is able to define himself against the Other by naming himself one thing and calling the Other something else. This argument is at the heart of Nietzsche's *Genealogy of Morals* and Foucault's research on the connection between discourse and power.[4] Symbolic representation is a way of translating and displacing the initial trauma of language onto different social relations by determining a debased and de-valorized object.

In Lacan's theory of the discourse of the master, the object (a) is placed in the position of being the lost product of the signifying chain:

$$\frac{S1}{\$}\text{-------->}\frac{S2}{(a)}$$

This can mean that in order for any discourse to stabilize itself, it has to produce its own object of exclusion.[5] As in Julia Kristeva's interpretation of abjection, this object is placed at the limits of the Symbolic and takes on the appearance of representing the lost Real.[6]

At the same time that the subject and the social system localizes all linguistic loss in the position of the debased object (a), there is also an attempt to deny this lack by creating a fetish that lacks nothing. The role of the feminine form in this structure is therefore split between being the object of horror and being the object of desired completeness and fulfillment. While it has been argued that Hollywood attempts to hide the abject object by idealizing the image of women, I would like to argue that a film like *Spellbound* offers a reversal of this structure. The male subject in this film becomes anxious whenever he is placed in front of the feminine object because this object is tied to the presentation of a certain absence. Furthermore, I will show how his horror of the abject feminine object is doubled by his horror of writing.

The Horror of Writing

What most often causes John Ballantine to become dizzy and "hysterical" are the moments that he stares at white surfaces with black lines. The first example of this is when Constance, the Ingrid Bergman character, traces the outline of a swimming pool on a white surface with her fork and John becomes immediately upset and starts to berate her. Then later on, he becomes bothered when he sees the dark lines on her white bathrobe and on her white bedspread. At a certain point, Constance will say "think of white, think of black lines." This will be connected to skis going down white snow, in a reference to the scene of murder.

I would argue that what most commentators of this movie have missed is the most obvious and repetitive symbolism of the film. Black lines on a white surface refers to writing, just as the title *Spellbound* can refer to both a trance and the act of spelling out something in language.[7] In this sense, John's horror is a horror of writing and feminine sexuality. Virtually, every time that Ballantine becomes anxious, he is with Constance, to whom he shows himself to be attracted.

In a pardigmatic scene, Constance etches with a fork on a white table cloth, the outline of a swimming pool, and in reaction to this drawing, Ballantine becomes extremely agitated. As many commentators have pointed out, the shape that Constance draws takes the form of a vagina.[8] This would indicate that this male character not only has a fear of writing, but that he also can not tolerate the sight of the female organ. We can therefore search for a Symbolic relation between writing and feminine sexuality.

On the most basic level, the link between writing and femininity can be related to the mutual representation of absence. Writing makes the absence of the Thing present, just as in Freud's theory, the vagina makes the absence of the phallus present for the male. The horror of writing is, in this sense, based on a horror of castration. This theme brings Hitchcock very close to an understanding of Derrida's *On Grammotology*.[9]

In his critique of the Western tradition's favoring of speech over writing, Derrida points out that the "exterior"

written letter appears to threaten the interiority of consciousness and self-presence. "Writing, the letter, the sensi-
ble inscription, has always been considered by Western
tradition as the body and matter external to the spirit, to
breath, to speech, and to the logos" (35). According to
Derrida, for a thinker like Rousseau, writing becomes a
"deadly supplement" that represents the artificiality of language and human culture (141–164).

Part of this fear of writing can be connected to the fact
that, in speech, the subject has to exist in the Real in order
to produce a discourse, but in writing, the subject of the
speech is often missing or absent. This dislocation of language from the subject can be called a "be-heading" or a "castration" since writing highlights the way that one can
produce a discourse without a controlling subject or cogito.
The fear of writing is thus, in part, a fear of losing control of
discourse and the ability to present oneself in the Real.

We can now read John Ballantine's horror of writing
and the feminine as a fear of losing his own sense of self and
control. Furthermore, using Silverman's argument about the
double structure of castration, we can posit that the equating
of the feminine organ with writing, represents the subject's
desire to displace his horror of linguistic castration onto the
female object. In the formation of this projection, the male
subject says to himself, "I am not castrated by language, but
she is anatomically castrated." Silverman adds that this
process allows the male subject to externalize the cause of
his anxiety, and therefore, he can flee from it by a phobic
avoidance (16).

Freud's Fetishism

Central to Silverman's argument is the idea that Freud
himself, in his theory of castration and fetishism, acts out his
own process of denial and projection:

> The malice Freud himself exhibits toward the female sub-
> ject in the course of his essay on anatomical difference—
> the "triumphant contempt" he encourages the male subject

to entertain for the "mutilated creature" who is the sexual other. This set of emotions attests to nothing so much as a successfully engineered projection, to the externalizing displacement onto the female subject of what the male cannot tolerate in himself: castration or lack. (16)

In other words, the entire theory of anatomical castration is based on a displacement of linguistic castration by the male subject, who this time happens to be Freud.

However, Silverman adds that because Freud describes the masculine encounter with the feminine lack as "uncanny," he must be aware that this traumatic experience refers to an earlier event. This is due to the fact that Freud himself insists that the "uncanny" relates to "that class of the frightening which leads back to what is known of old and long familiar" (quoted in Silverman, 17). Castration is here tied to a process of repetition that relates to an earlier experience of loss and absence.

This double theory of castration and repetition ties together Freud's theories of the death drive, the Oedipus Complex, and the castration complex. We shall see how the death drive is based on the subject's attempt to master and displace loss by repeating it on a Symbolic level. More so, the Oedipus Complex, which explains why the subject must give up his or her first object (the mother) in order to identify with the father, is centered on the subject's alienation in the Symbolic order and separation from the Real. Furthermore, Freud argues that the resolution of the Oedipus complex is determined by the threat of castration that we have just attached to the production and the projection of linguistic loss.

The death drive, the Oedipus Complex, and the castration complex, all seem to tell and retell the same story; as human beings we lose ourselves in language and then we deny and project this loss onto others. But if this narrative is tied to the production of masculine subjectivity, how can we posit a theory of feminine subjectivity? I will attempt to outline an answer to this question after I analyze these structures in *Spellbound* from the perspective of the male subject.

The Lacking Subject in Spellbound

In the film, John Ballantine is a man who has lost his memory and believes that he has murdered his own doctor and then assumed the doctor's identity. Since he does not know who he is, he can be compared to the subject of the unconscious that Lacan defines as being a "hole" or a "lack" in the Symbolic structure of the Other.[10] The subject has no signifier or place in the Other, because on the level of one's unconscious, one clings to the Real, which by definition is impossible to Symbolize. Lacan thus posits a fundamental rejection (foreclosure) of the Symbolic order for every subject of the unconscious.

Yet, as subjects of language, we do find a way of placing ourselves in this Other realm. In Freudian theory, the central mechanism for this process of Symbolic interpellation is identification. In John Ballantine's case, since he has no self-identity, he takes on the identity of another person, the doctor who he thinks he has killed. In other words, identification with the Other is based on the lack of identity of the subject.

John Ballantine will say himself that when he looks in the mirror he sees nothing, not even a reflection. He has no identity, no memory and no image—he is reduced to being a letter that others will attempt to read. For the only thing that he knows about himself is that his initials are J. B. When he escapes to New York, he takes on the name John Brown, which once again indicates his need to find a signifier in the Other and to replace a pair of letters with a spoken name. In the structure of the repetition and displacement of loss, he desires to find a second name in order to make up for the loss of his original name. He also desires to move from an identity that is determined by writing (his initials, J. B.) to a form of identification that is founded on speech.

In Freud's theory, the process of identification is always tied to the loss of an object-choice.[11] In the classical structure of the resolution of the Oedipus Complex, the boy gives up his mother as a love-object and identifies with the desire of the father. In John Ballantine's case, we can say that he has given up his original object by killing his doctor, at the same time that he has identified with him.[12] This connection between identification and murder points not only to the resolution of the Oedipus Complex, but it also relates to Freud's theory of the primal horde and the foundations of civilization.

In *Totem and Taboo*, Freud argues that social laws and morality were formed out of a reaction to the original murder of an all-powerful primal father figure.[13] After a group of brothers got together and killed their father so they could sleep with their sisters, they became guilty and set up laws against incest and murder. In order to commemorate the murdered father and to organize the different kinship relations that prevent incest, the brothers defined certain taboos and determined a group totem.

This historical theory can be read as an allegory of the way that every subject and society rejects its relation to the Real in order to find an identity on the Symbolic level. The flip side of this is that there is always a part of the repressed Real that returns and thus threatens to undermine the Symbolic order. In John Ballantine's case, he has killed his father figure and has identified with this Symbolic Other, but he is constantly menaced by the return of a repressed primal scene.

Ballantine is haunted by the guilt that he killed his brother by accident when he was a child. In the flashback to this scene, we find him sliding down a bannister and pushing his brother, who flies off and lands on a spike. John Ballantine, then, was to have repressed this event and only become aware of it once the scene was repeated by his doctor skiing off a cliff.

In Freud's theory, we can say that the initial scene only becomes traumatic through its repetition, because only through repetition does a Real event take on Symbolic signification. In other words, the initial scene takes on its traumatic effect after the fact, when the subject has the ability to reinterpret it and give it meaning. It is repetition then, and not the Real event, that is traumatic for the subject.[14]

This theory of the trauma after the fact is later formulated by Freud through his theory of the death drive. In *Beyond the Pleasure Principle*, Freud points out that when some one continuously dreams of a horrible event or a child acts out a difficult experience in a game, the subject is attempting to master the event by moving from a position of passivity to one of activity in the Symbolic repetition of the act.[15] Furthermore, Freud argues that in anxiety dreams and children's games, what is generated in order to bind the event is a level of anxiety that was missing during the first event (13). One could argue that this is one of the functions of the suspense or horror film. By representing a scene or by seeing the traumatic scene represented in a safe environment, anxiety is generated that now can be attached to infantile and unconscious events.

In Hitchcock's rendition of this theory, it is guilt that was absent or repressed in the first event that becomes active in the repetition of the second event. Gregory Peck's character believes that he is guilty of pushing his doctor off the cliff in order to generate the guilt that he may or may not have felt about his brother's death. It is therefore in the Symbolic repetition of the scene that the guilt is generated, which will bind and reinterpret the original scene.

If we now return to Silverman's argument about the double structure of castration, we can state that the first event of linguistic loss only becomes traumatic once it is repeated and projected onto the place of the Other. However, we now have to reconcile the relation between at least four traumatic scenes of castration and loss in *Spellbound*. First we have the primal loss caused by linguistic castration, then we have the real loss of the subject's brother, next we have the loss caused by the death of the doctor, and finally we have the absence that is represented by writing and femininity. Each loss seems to build on and displace the previous loss/losses. Yet, I believe that we can give a structure to this displacement of lack by first distinguishing between the repetition of loss on the level of the death drive and the return of loss on the level of the unconscious.

With the death drive, the subject is able to control the object that causes anxiety by submitting it to a process of Symbolic representation. Thus, John Ballantine deals with the loss of his brother and the loss of his own identity by pretending that he is the one who really pushed the doctor off the cliff. By repeating the primal scene, he is able to attach the initial trauma to a scene of Symbolic repetition that serves to efface from memory the initial event. In a way, he says to himself, "No, I did not kill my brother, no I am not alienated by language, but I did kill the doctor and take on his identity."

However, this attempt to efface the primal scene fails and he becomes a victim to his unconscious desire to return to the Real. The Real here is both the realm of the lost maternal object (his horror of Constance's presence) and the insistence of writing in the unconscious. We must not forget that all that Ballantine knows about himself is that his initials are J. B. and that he has a horror of seeing black lines on a white surface. As I argued above, we can say that these black lines represent writing and the presentation of absence. More so, I would add that his fear of writing is based on a fear of traces, memories, and tracks.

In this film, Hitchcock reminds us that it is because we have memory that we can retain elements of the past and therefore we are open to being plagued by our past failures or crimes. The existence of writing means that traces are always left behind in the textuality of the unconscious. In fact, Freud himself will describe the memory system as a series of traces and tracks that relate to each other.[16] If a trace is the mark of an absence, it is the track which places the traces together. In Hitchcock's imagery, it is indeed the train track that often appears as the symbol of connections and traces—a visual representation of the memory system of writing.

Furthermore, the crime story is the perfect allegory for the process of writing and memory because it is based on the desire to hunt down traces and to follow tracks back to the place of an initial crime. Just as in psychoanalysis, when the analyst helps the analysand to reconstruct the past through present unconscious formations, the detective attempts to reconstruct the scene of the crime by looking for clues and unconscious faults.

Dream Reading

In order to discover what John Ballantine has repressed, Constance will have to interpret one of his dreams. In other words, Hitchcock places the truth of the subject within the domain of an unconscious formation. It is in this scene of dream interpretation and Symbolic reading that the ethical dimension of the film will be presented.

In the dream, we first see eyes on a curtain that are then cut by a man with a pair of large scissors. I would like to read this image as representing Hitchcock's indication of the way that the subject of vision is cut or barred by the system of Symbolic representation. Here, Hitchcock displays an awareness of the destructive nature of film representation where the structure of the signifier cuts off the field of vision. He also depicts with the help of Salvador Dali, the way that the subject of the unconscious is projected and perceived in dreams as lacking its place.

Later on in the dream, we see a card game where one of the players is dealt a hand of blank cards. We can read this as the pictorial representation of the subject that has no signifier or identity. As Lacan will state, the subject of the unconscious is a subject without a name or identification (26). Furthermore, the dealer in the card game wears a mask, which hides his face—this is another subject who is not only without an identity, but is also without an image.

Later on in the dream, we see a broken wheel, this could refer to Hitchcock's usual reference to the film reel in the form of a wheel. The broken wheel then represents the broken camera or the failures of representation. Perhaps, we can read this dream symbol as an indication of the director's own sense of guilt for his attempt to Symbolize the Real. After all, the film starts with a quote from Shakespeare, "The fault is not in the stars but in ourselves." This might indicate that it is not his actor's fault (the stars), but his own—he cannot help but destroy or block light through the process of filming. In fact, the wheel will be read as a symbol of a revolver, thus linking the film reel to a gun.

In the second to last scene, this connection between death and representation becomes apparent. While Constance is confronting the director with her interpretation of J. B.'s dream, which proves that the director is the Real murderer, he takes out a gun and begins to aim it at her. Then the camera takes on the subjective view of the pistol. At first the camera

gun aims at the Other but then it turns around on the subject and the director shoots himself. Here, the author is
clearly dead—the director has even murdered himself.

This scene where the camera becomes a gun shows
Hitchcock's' profound awareness of the workings of the death
drive. The destructive nature of the Symbolic order is now
represented in the Real. As Freud and Lacan have argued,
the subject of the unconscious always attempts to push
abstract Symbolic concepts and structures into the Real by
experiencing them on the level of a projected perception. It is
through this process, I would argue, that Hitchcock presents
an ethics of representation by revealing the inner workings
of the death drive.

At the end of this scene, Constance convinces the director not to kill her because he could plead insanity for the first
crime, but not for the second one. Once again, this indicates
that guilt only comes about through the repetition of the act.
Hitchcock's universe is thus an ethical one, based on the
themes of truth, memory, guilt, and revelation. But it is also
an aesthetic one. After all, Constance determines the truth of
the crime by interpreting a dream that centers around both
the question of murder and the process of representation.

Feminine Subjectivity

Up to this point, I have concentrated on the structure of
masculine subjectivity as it relates to the death drive and
the unconscious. If we now turn things around, and we
attempt to determine what this film says about feminine
subjectivity, we are left with two choices. Either we can discuss the way that Ballantine is "feminized" by his encounter
with the female object or we can attempt to articulate the
film from Constance's perspective.

In the opening of *Spellbound*, Constance plays the role
of a desexualized psychoanalyst, who is compared to being as
lifeless as a "textbook." A fellow psychiatrist calls her this,
because she will not let him seduce her. From this male's
perspective, a woman can only be compared to writing, if she
denies her own sexuality and clings to abstract knowledge.

This split between sexuality and book smarts is a classic division in Hitchcock's work, yet as this film progresses, Constance will become all the more sensual, the more she learns and knows.[17] After all, it is Constance who acts as the detective-psychoanalyst in the film. It is therefore her search and her desire to know that directs the flow of the action. In the central scene where she finally confronts the director with her interpretation of Ballantine's dream by using her analytic techniques, she becomes the one that challenges the dominant male figure. Dr. Murchison is not only the real murderer, but he also represents a chain of directors that stretches from himself, to the real Dr. Edwardes, to the fake Dr. Edwardes, and ultimately to Hitchcock himself.[18]

Constance's effective reading of John Ballantine's unconscious therefore puts her in a position to undermine every male in the film, including Hitchcock. Perhaps, the male director can only shoot himself at the end because the female subject has gained access to his own repressed desire. By reading this aspect of the film as an allegory of feminine power, we can help to break the spell that has entrapped so many of its readers and viewers into seeing this film as a bad primer on psychoanalysis or as a monological specula-tion on the "moral universe."[19]

By centering itself on an ethics of desire and not on a morality of social control, *Spellbound* not only chronicles Constance's sexual awakening, but it also points to an empowerment of feminine desire and discourse. Of course this argument will anger all of the people who are invested in reading Hitchcock's work as a misogynist's attempt to con-trol women. Yet, this very supposition of control is based on a denial of the inability of any subject to totally direct and master the flow of discourse and language. I would like to insist that to read Hitchcock as a pure misogynist is to con-stitute an authorial fetish by denying linguistic lack and set-ting up in its place an idealized version of directorial intent.

It is clear that this fetishistic idealization of authorship is at play in Thomas Hyde's essay, "The Moral Universe of Hitchcock and *Spellbound*," when he argues that: "One would hardly want to rank *Spellbound* (1945) as one of Hitchcock's richest or most perfectly conceived films. Even the Master himself . . . told Frances Truffaut in his interview book that it was "just another manhunt story wrapped up in pseudo-psychoanalysis"" (153). By taking the word of the "Master," this critic falls prey to Hitchcock's own attempt at being self-parodic.[20] More so, the idea of ranking his films in relation to their richness and perfect conception reveals an ideology of the "perfect form" that only a "Great Man" can realize.

The ideology of the unified control of the master director-auteur is related to the moralistic psychology that runs throughout Hyde's commentary. This critic believes that the central plot of the film shows that "ultimately more absorbing than the determination of John's innocence is their personal transformation—becoming integrated within themselves and so redeemed for each other" (154). It is therefore the integration of the self that Hyde holds out to be the most redeeming quality. Of course this state of integration can only be established by denying the disruptive aspects of language and sexuality.

In her book *Male Subjectivity at the Margins*, Kaja Silverman outlines some of the reasons why the search for masculine mastery and integration is always produced against the threat of language and social history. "The male subject's aspirations to mastery and sufficiency are undermined from many directions—by the Law of Language, which founds subjectivity on a void; by the castration crisis; by sexual, economic, and racial oppression; and by the traumatically inassimilable nature of certain historical events."[21] We can say that John Ballantine fits very well into this structure of marginalized masculinity. This male subject identifies with the void or lack that is caused by the imposition of the Symbolic order, at the same time that he displays a horror of femininity and writing. In the doubled nature of his bi-textuality, Ballantine both rejects and identifies with the feminine resistance to the phallo-logocentric aspects of discourse. From this perspective, we can say that this male subject identifies with the form of feminine writing that he also rejects.

Silverman argues that *Spellbound* is one of many films that were made at the end of World War II and that all have as a central theme a man who has been castrated by the war and a woman who takes on the active role of directing the narrative (54). She posits that if in the classical version of the film narrative, the male subject directs the helpless female object, in these post-World War II movies, the woman is shown to be active, while the male figure is either scarred or impotent. This lack of activity and phallic control by the masculine subject is often connected in these films to some wound that the subject received in a war. In fact, in *Spellbound*, we learn that Ballantine's plane was shot down during the war and that his body was badly burned. Thus, his wound represents the way that his own body has been marked by castration, and therefore he is placed in the feminine role of embodying the masculine lack.

What I am arguing here is that Ballantine himself represents an aspect of feminine subjectivity in the film. He is plagued by a horror of representation because he has been traumatized by the Symbolic order. This feminine identification can in part explain why he cannot control the death drive and actively represses his own unconscious; every attempt that he makes to repeat and thus repress or project his own unconscious feelings of lack, result in a return of this lack in the Real. If feminine and feminized subjects are dominated by lack, can we not infer that part of this domination is due to their enforced inability to reinterpret and project absence through the putting into play of the death drive and the signifying chain? I believe this is precisely what Luce Irigary is articulating when she states that:

> It is not that she lacks some "master signifier" or that none is imposed upon her, but rather that access to a signifying economy, to the coining of signifiers, is difficult or even impossible for her because she remains an outsider, herself (a) subject to their norms.[22]

Returning to our discussion of the discourse of the master, we can say that women do have access to master signifiers (S1), but rarely do they control the signifying chains (S2) that are used to socially determine objects of exclusion and abjection.

However, in the radical nature of Hitchcock's film, Constance is the one who interprets and gives meaning to lack and absence. In fact, her control of the signifying chain almost causes the loss of her own life. This becomes evident when the director says to her that she may be a good analyst, but she is a "very stupid woman," because he now has to kill her for discovering his secret. She then convinces him not to kill her, so she is able to survive with the knowledge that she gains. In this sense, Constance challenges Tania Modleski's thesis that in Hitchcock's films, the woman who knows too much is punished and violently attacked.[23]

As Constance becomes attached to the control of discourse and the discovery of truth; Ballantine becomes associated with the feminine insistence on writing and lack. In this crossing of traditional gender roles and linguistic positions, Hitchcock highlights the way that men identify with the loss of language and discourse that they project onto women. In this structure, the male subject becomes feminized the moment that he identifies with the bi-textual presence of absence.

The Ethics of Bi-Textuality

Just as Freud posits a fundamental state of bisexuality and polymorphous perversity, we can assert that there is a polymorphous level of film. Our question then becomes how do films and subjects become en-gendered? The processes of abjection, identification, and fetishistic reinterpretation all point to the ways that male subjects take on certain sexual and social positions, but do these same formations account for feminine subjectivity? It would seem that since the dominant order of discourse inherently discriminates against women in favor of men, women are left with two fundamental positions. Either they take control and reinterpret their own master signifiers, or they attempt to establish a new form of discourse, something like a structured multiplicity or a bi-textuality.

I have been arguing that both tasks can be accomplished at once, by the radical attempt at rereading and reinterpreting the masculine signifiers, whose constant need for reiteration and reaffirmation point to the unstable grounds that support them.[24] Psychoanalysis, deconstruction, and poetry all provide strong tools for the dismantling and upsetting of the monological masculine discourse. Yet, these tools will go unused if they are not affirmed and put into play by people who are committed to heterogenous life-styles and methods of interaction.

The first step to this affirmation of the multiple, may be the acknowledgement that none of us are in control of language and that we are all alienated in the discourse of the Other. The next step is to be vigilant against the attempt to displace our own linguistic lack onto others through the process of abjection. We must reinterpret our world in order to free it from singular interpretations and not reestablish fetishistic forms of denial.

Spellbound allows us to see how masculine subjects attempt to escape from their own awareness of linguistic and sexual loss by projecting lack and discourse castration onto women. However, Hitchcock effectively shows how this process of projection fails and that the result of this failure is the return of repressed feelings of loss and alienation. In this sense, the woman who is presented as the embodiment of absence only serves to heighten the male subject's own sense of lack. In the bi-textual nature of his films, Hitchcock displays both the way that the Symbolic death drive attempts to displace loss and the way that loss returns on the level of the ethical unconscious.

3

Rebecca, Repetition, and the Circulation of Feminine Desire: Judith Butler and the Materiality of the Letter

In the previous chapters, I have concentrated on the opposition between the masculine realm of sexual representation and feminine aspects of subjectivity and writing. In this binary structure, the masculine control of discourse and the Symbolic death drive is resisted by a form of unconscious feminine writing that refuses to be contained by the heterosexual constraints of the phallo-logocentric order. I have been using the term bi-textuality in order to tie together the presence of diverse forms of sexuality and language that counter the dominant symbolic order. In this chapter, I will examine the way that the circulation of desire between women undermines the masculine heterosexist death drive.

Rebecca and The Death Drive

The film *Rebecca* begins with a long voice-over spoken by an unidentified female, which I will now quote in its entirety:

> Last night I dreamt I went to Manderley again. It seemed to me I stood by the iron-gate leading to the drive and for a while, I could not enter for the way was barred to me. Then, like all dreamers, I was possessed of a sudden with supernatural powers and passed like a spirit through the barrier before me.

The drive wound away in front of me, twisting and turning as it always had done, but as I advanced, I was aware that a change had come upon it. Nature had come into her own again and little by little had encroached upon the drive with long tenacious fingers.

On and on wound the poor thread that had once been our drive and finally, there was Manderley. Manderley, secretive and silent—time could not mar the perfect symmetry of those walls.

Moonlight can play odd tricks upon the fancy and suddenly it seemed to me that light came from the windows and then a cloud came upon the moon and hovered an instant like a dark hand before a face. The illusion went with it. I looked upon a desolate shell with no whisper of the past about its staring walls. We can never go back to Manderley again, that much is certain. But sometimes, in my dreams, I do go back to those strange days of my life, which began for me in the South of France.[1]

In the opening lines of this speech, we learn that this female voice returns to something called "Manderley" in her dreams. It is thus on the level of her unconscious that she has access to this location. Furthermore, we can hear in the name "Manderley" the word "Man" and this unconscious connection links this female voice to her return to a masculine domain.

This female subject tells us that at first her access was barred to this place—as a feminine subject she could not enter the masculine home. However, through a special power of her unconscious, her "spirit" broke through the barrier. I would like to read this passage as indicating that one of the ways that a female voice is allowed to enter into the home of a masculine controlled place is by detaching its voice from its body.

This concept of a disembodied voice is discussed at length in Kaja Silverman's book *The Acoustic Mirror*.[2] Silverman argues that in the classic structure of film representation, we often find the situation where a masculine voice determines the movement of a female body. Furthermore, Silverman argues that men in our culture have been increasingly connected to the pure realm of linguistic power that is detached from vision and the body: "Over the past two centuries, the male subject has increasingly dissociated himself from the visible, attempting to thereby to align himself with a symbolic order within which power has become more and more dispersed and dematerial" (26). This theory implies that in order to take on the God-like characteristics of an all-seeing and all-knowing paternal figure, male subjects in film disconnect their selves and voices from their visible bodies.

An extreme form of this opposition between masculine speech and female body-images can be found in the masculine voice-over that allows the bodiless male voice to float over the action of the film. "The voice-over is privileged to the degree that it transcends the body. Conversely it loses power and authority with every corporeal encroachment" (49). In this structure, power is determined by the male's ability to dissociate his voice from the materiality of language and the body.

I would like to argue that *Rebecca* offers an inversion of this traditional connection between the female body and the masculine voice. In this film, it is not a masculine voice that controls the action and the movements of the female body; rather, it is a certain detached female voice that will enter into the body of a masculine space.

As the original voice-over states, nature has encroached on the previously cleared drive that leads to Manderley, just as the female voice has broken through its iron-gate. One can attach this encroaching nature to the movement of a feminine presence that threatens the workings of the masculine death drive.[3] The drive itself is a path that is cut into a natural field, thus allowing for the "progress" of civilization. In Lacan's theory, the drive is the structure of language that accounts for the way that humans cut into the natural realm in order to hollow out a space for Symbolism and utility.

In Freud's application of the death drive to children's games, he shows how the subject of language is able to separate himself or herself from the "natural" realm of Real things, maternal desire, and his or her own specular image. From this perspective, we can argue that the classic structure of film narration serves to reenact the death drive's overcoming of the natural forces of the Real and the mother in a gendered structure. In the traditional Hollywood film, men affirm their symbolic power and control over language by rendering the female subject speechless and by connecting her presence to the materiality of her body. This structure is evident in the beginning of *Rebecca*, where we constantly see the leading male figure, Max, order and command his timid female companion.

Max's way of linguistically controlling his future wife at the start of the film is coupled with his attempt to humiliate her and treat her like a child. When he realizes that he must propose to her or lose her, he declares: "I'm asking you to marry me, you little fool!" This strange marriage proposal is delivered while Max is hidden in the bathroom. In this structure, the viewing audience only hears Max's voice while they watch his future wife's physical reactions. By separating this domineering male's voice from his bodily presence, Hitchcock is able to visibly reinforce the power that the male subject receives from the separation of his language from the materiality of his body.

Max's control of the linguistic realm continues as he and his new bride approach the intimidating mansion, Manderley. In response to his wife's growing anxiety and feelings of inferiority, Max reassures her by stating: "Don't worry, you won't have to say a word." This phrase shows Max's clear desire to remove this female subject from the Symbolic order of words and power. However, as soon as the newlyweds enter into Manderley, they discover that this mansion is controlled by two dominant female powers—the housemaid, Mrs. Danvers, and the presence of Max's dead wife, Rebecca.

As in the opening voice-over, Rebecca's invisible presence determines the unfolding of the narrative. Even though she is dead and no longer physically present, Rebecca's absence cannot be forgotten. One of the main ways that her presence is maintained is through the insistence and repetition of the letter R.[4] Wherever the second Mrs. de Winter goes in her new home, she is forced to encounter the first Mrs. de Winter's initials. As in the case of *The Lady Vanishes*, this film uses letters and other material traces in order to mark the return of the repressed female subject.

The patriarchal figure, Max, has killed his first wife but he cannot completely efface the presence of her existence. We can interpret the letter R as the symbol of both the return of the repressed and the Real of a female figure who refuses to vanish beneath the masculine signifier and death drive. This reemergence of a repressed female presence is further accented in the film when the original Mrs. de Winter's body is found at the bottom of the sea.

Doubling this effacement and return of the first Mrs. de Winter, we find the second Mrs. de Winter's attempt to take on the role of the original love-object. The idea that she is only a replacement for the first wife becomes apparent by the fact that we never learn her name in the film. She is another one of Hitchcock's subjects who has no signifier and thus she must take on the name of the Other. As an unconscious subject without a name or an identity, she can only hope to reiterate the signifier and role of another woman. Her task in the film is to materialize and give body to the immaterial presence of Rebecca's absence. Yet, this process of materializing the absent female subject is precisely what Max and the patriarchal Symbolic order is trying to prevent.

In the structure of this film, Max turns to the second Mrs. de Winter in order to forget the first Mrs. de Winter. His need to replace one female subject with another repeats the classical Oedipal structure where the male subject searches for a woman who will act as a Symbolic substitute for his Real mother.[5] The paradox of this structure is that the female subject must represent the absence of the mother and not her presence. In other words, if the substitute love-object is too much like the mother, the male subject will suffer a sense of guilt and incestuous shame.

This paradoxical nature of male desire is doubled by the contradictory nature of the linguistic order. Lacan argues that the Symbolic order of language is set up to allow us to separate from the material world; yet, language is also called to represent the Real. In the masculine structure of the death drive, words represent the absence or loss of the Real; but unconscious desire seeks to refind the Real thing that is effaced by language. Once again, the contradictions of the love relation doubles the contradiction of the

relations of language and the Real. We have language to forget the Real, yet language calls us to constantly long for a
return of the absent object. Hitchcock's solution to this problem is to represent a form of language that is both material
and transcendent. In other terms, he turns words into things
and in this act of bi-textuality, he is able to collapse the difference between the feminine body and the masculine signifier.

This dual nature of bi-textuality also accounts for the
way that the second Mrs. de Winter undermines the classic
structure of Oedipal love by refusing to play the role of the
female surrogate for the lost mother-object. In the masculine
version of Oedipal sexuality, the substitute female love-object
is supposed to help the male subject efface the evidence of
his first love, the mother. However, the second Mrs. de
Winter attaches herself to the process of memory instead of
that of forgetting. On one of her drives with Max, the future
Mrs. de Winter states, "I wish there could be an invention
that would bottle up a memory like a perfume and it never
faded, never got stale. Then when I wanted to I could uncork
the bottle and live the memory all over again." This female
subject would like to keep her memories in a bottle just like
Max has placed Rebecca in a bottle or boat at the bottom of
the sea.

In response to the feminine desire for memory, Max
declares that, "Sometimes, you know, those little bottles contain demons that have a way of popping out at you just when
you're trying most desperately to forget." This statement
prefigures the rediscovery of the already buried Rebecca
towards the end of the film. Max has tried to bury and
repress his first object of desire into the depths of his unconscious, but she keeps on popping up when he least expects it.
His anger at his companion is precisely an anger focused on
her desire to remember and remind.

As in other films, Hitchcock connects the emergence of
truth to the return of a repressed unconscious element. In
our binary reading of the film, the male-figure would like to
forget the primal scene or original object, while the female
figure wants to retain it. However, at the same time, the
feminine love-object is used to erase or forget the past. This
latter use of the female substitute is apparent when Max

says to his second wife, "You blotted out the past for me, more than all of the bright lights in Monte Carlo." This statement could indicate that this male subject turns to another female in order to forget about his love and the eventual murder of his original object-choice (the mother).

The Other Side of Freud

What this film shows is perhaps the other side of Freud's essays on the conditions of the love-object. In his discussion of masculine desire, Freud argues that for a man, the love-object must be (1) desired by a third party, (2) have the reputation of being a virgin, (3) remind the subject of the mother, and (4) not remind the subject of the mother (232–235). All of these paradoxes come under the heading of the Madonna-Whore Complex. The male subject wants his love-object to be sexually knowledgeable but still be pure. He also wants her to be desired by other men, yet he wants to be the first man. Likewise, she should remind him of his mother but not be too much like her.

The second Mrs. de Winter fits all of these traits of the masculine object-choice. At first, Max's relatives think that she must be a show girl, but she shows herself to be inexperienced. She is also nothing like Rebecca, but once she changes her clothing and puts on a wig, she becomes just like Rebecca. In other words, through masquerade she takes on the role of the original object. However, because she reminds Max too much of his first love, he can only respond to her with fear and anger.

But what would happen if we read this story from the other angle, not from the position of masculine subjectivity, but from the perspective of feminine desire? The other side of the Madonna-Whore complex and the Oedipal structure of desire is that the female subject has to position herself in a space outside of these contradictory binary alternatives. Being neither a whore nor a Madonna, she must seek a presence in the form of an absolute difference from the masculine representations of femininity. This relationship between desire, repetition, femininity, and identity receives an intricate reading in Judith Butler's book *Bodies That Matter*.[6] In this text, Butler discusses the way that sexuality is materialized through the processes of exclusion, foreclosure, reiteration, and performance.

On the level of foreclosure, sexuality is defined by the way that the subject of the unconscious is rejected by and rejects the normative discourse of sexuality. In order to remain on the level of the Real, the unconscious bisexual subject has to resist all forms of social and Symbolic regulation. Likewise, society itself has to delimit what acts and subjectivities are considered to be taboo and unrepresentable.

On the other hand, the allowable forms of sexual identification and activity only become intelligible through their constant reiteration and performative reproduction. Since, ultimately, the subject has no signifier of sexual identification (Freud's theory of universal bi-sexuality), sexual identity has to be constructed and repetitively acted out. In the case of *Rebecca*, the second wife has no name for herself, and so she can only take on the name of the Other. However, because she can never quite fit this signifier, nor the roles that it implies, she must continually repeat and re-iterate her identification as Mrs. de Winter.

One of the ways that feminine desire repeats and is circulated in *Rebecca* is through Mrs. Danvers, the maid. She continuously acts as the third party who mediates the feminine desire between Rebecca and the second Mrs. de Winter. After all, it is Mrs. Danvers who tricks the second wife into masquerading like the first one, by suggesting that she dress like the woman in the hallway portrait. In this way, it is a woman who directs another woman's desire towards a representation of a third woman.[7]

The nature of desire in this film counters the traditional structure where a masculine figure directs the female subject towards the ideal representation of another woman. In the normative Symbolic order, we can say with Lacan, the desire of the subject is the desire of the Other, and, therefore, every subject's desire is socially mediated and determined by the dominant (patriarchal) powers. Yet, I am arguing that in *Rebecca*, the circulation of desire is articulated in a lesbian homosocial structure.[8]

We know in the film that Mrs. Danvers loved and idealized the missing Rebecca, but what we also learn that she had a special place in her lady's bedroom. Every night before Rebecca would go to sleep, Mrs. Danvers would comb her hair and then direct her towards the bed where her translucent nightgown would lay. Mrs. Danvers knit it herself; and, in order to show its sheerness to the second wife, she sticks her hand beneath it. This hand beneath the see-through veil is a reversal of the opening voice-over's description of the cloud in front of the moon being like a hand in front of one's face. Furthermore, these two descriptions of visibility and invisibility are related to a third scene, where Max's head blocks the path of the film projector leading to the screen.

I would like to read these three examples as an allegory of the relationship between heterosexual desire and lesbian desire. In the case of Max standing in front of the projector, the male figure blocks the light that would have projected the image of the female figure on the screen for another female subject. Here, the feminine control of the mirror stage of identification is disrupted by the male figure. On the other hand, in the case of Mrs. Danvers' hand beneath the nightgown, there is no blocking of the female image—one woman can see another woman, because there is no man in the way.

In the scene where Mrs. Danvers first shows off Rebecca's see-through nightgown, she gets the second wife to reenact and reiterate the first wife's nightly routine. While the second Mrs. de Winter looks into the mirror, Mrs. Danvers begins to comb her hair. In this structure, the narcissistic relation of the second wife staring into the mirror is combined with a lesbian eroticism (Mrs. Danvers is touching her hair). Furthermore, the mirror that is being looked into is Rebecca's mirror, and thus the specular image is being framed by the look of another woman.

This doubling of female desire within the structure of the narcissistic relation points to one of the difficulties of Lacan's theory of the mirror stage and Freud's theory of the Oedipus Complex. Even if the subject falls in love with its own ideal image, this process of mirroring is most often doubled by the love that the subject has for the image of the ideal loving mother.[9] In classical psychoanalytic theory, we are led to believe that the first ideal object of love for the boy and the girl is the mother. It is then the role of the resolution of the Oedipus Complex to change this object-choice so that the boy identifies with the father and loves the mother through the father's desire. In the more complicated structure of feminine desire, the little girl must give up her love for the mother and take the father as the love object. This means that her love starts out to be a lesbian love while the boy's desire starts out to be a heterosexual one. Lesbian desire is therefore at the heart of the analytic conception of the feminine Oedipus Complex, yet this heart is rarely discussed.[10]

The lesbian structure of homosocial feminine desire is apparent throughout this movie. When the film begins, the second Mrs. de Winter is in the employment of her mother figure, Mrs. Van Hopper. She tells Max that her official role is to be a companion and that the term "companion" means "a friend of the bosom." This relationship, between "The Great Lady" and her assistant, is thus already defined by a certain circulation of lesbian desire.

When Max proposes to his future wife, he tells her that she must choose between going with Mrs. Van Hopper to New York or going to Manderley with him. In other words, her choice is between a woman-to-woman relationship or a man-to-woman one. In this structure, she must give up her lesbian relationship with her mother figure in order to accept a heterosexual relationship with a father figure. The female subject, thus, does not only have to separate from the mother and the Real in order to accede to the male-dominated Symbolic structure, but she also has to give up all of her lesbian desires.

The absence of the discourse on lesbian desire is figured in the film by the dominant presence of Rebecca's absence. Starting from the mysterious voice-over, Rebecca is continuously hovering above the film's structure and narration. Tania Modleski, who does discuss the structure of feminine desire in this film, points out that Rebecca is placed in the position of the all-knowing, all-seeing, absent Other or God figure in the film. "She is actually posited within the diegesis as all-seeing—as for example when Mrs. Danvers asks the terrified heroine if she thinks the dead come back to watch the living and says that she sometimes thinks Rebecca comes back to watch the new couple" (52). The foreclosed feminine presence and its correlative lesbian desire, which has been repressed by the male structure of the film, returns in the form of a spirit, just as Freud posited that the dead return in the structure of animism.[11]

Modleski points out that this power of the dead feminine presence is emphasized in two scenes: the first scene occurs when the new wife receives a phone call and she states that Mrs. de Winter is dead (even though she is Mrs. de Winter), and the second event occurs when we see the reenactment of the central crime from the subjective angle of the missing Rebecca (53). However, if Rebecca does play the role of some absent yet present God, she needs the materiality of the second Mrs. de Winter in order to sustain her presence.

In this sense, the abstract concept of the woman, which Lacan claims does not exist, needs to be materialized through different performative activities. According to Judith Butler's reading of Julia Kristeva in her *Bodies That Matter*, "the materiality of the spoken signifier, the vocalization of sound, is already a psychic effort to reinstall and recapture a lost maternal body" (69). I would add that in *Rebecca*, the absence of the first woman is simultaneously recovered by the presence of another woman and the material traces that she has left behind. Once again, we find here the conjunction of femininity and the material trace.

The question of feminine desire becomes one of representation and the materiality of sexuality. How can one woman become a woman if "The Woman" does not exist, and she is only a construction of a male phantasy? As Butler has pointed out, this question of the materiality of sex is at the heart of the general question of the materiality of language:

> Signs work be appearing (visibly, aurally), and appearing through material means, although what appears only signifies by virtue of those non-phenomenal relations, i.e., relations of differentiation, which tacitly structure and propel signification itself (68).

In Lacanian terms, this passage indicates that the Symbolic can only function by returning to the Real, although the Real itself has no Symbolic signification. Likewise, sexual identity is always structured by Symbolic relations of difference, yet those relations still need to be materialized in the Real.

In the case of *Rebecca*, the Symbolic themes of the lost mother, repetition, the lost Real, and foreclosed lesbian desire are all materialized through the production of non-signifying elements. Rebecca's presence is sustained not only by the presence of the second Mrs. de Winter, but also by the insistence of the letter *R* and the black dog, Jaspers, who is always sniffing the places where Rebecca had been. These two elements, the letter and the dog, both are signifying in the sense that they remind one of an absent person, yet at the same time they cannot communicate or signify on their own. The dog and the letter cannot speak or converse, however, their brute presence says something essential.

I would like to insist that these material reminders represent a fundamental element of Hitchcock's and Lacan's aesthetics and ethics: elements that represent a lack or failure of communication end up communicating the most. According to Thomas Cohen, memory itself is structured by this paradoxical nature of the materiality of language:

> Memory appears as the machinal enforcer of mimesis out of which the ideological closure of identification occurs, yet as a machine of repeated re-marking, it is also that which breaks up or destroys mimesis when figures, syllables, sounds, letters, and visual puns or objects emerge through repetition. (227)

This argument indicates that the insistent repetition of the meaningless letter *R* in *Rebecca*, points to both the possibility and impossibility of memory. By concentrating on the letter, we dissolve the word and undermine all attempts of signification. Yet, Lacan argues that language reveals itself only in as much as it fails and allows for the emergence of letters in the unconscious.[12] We only get to know the subject's true desire, when he or she makes a slip or faulty action and thus circumvents the social censure.

If, as I am arguing, a central part of Lacan's and Hitchcock's work revolves around writing and the letter, why are both of these aspects so often ignored? Cohen begins to formulate a response to this question by asserting that, "Hitchcockian writing seems largely untracked today in the criticism because it ceaselessly interrupts the pretense which the spectator desires—identification, the appearance of subjectivity, the wholeness of the body" (227). Since, the possibility of identification and the illusion of the totality of the body is founded on the ego's ability to appropriate the discourse of the Other and to establish stable forms of representation, the insistence of dispersed letters threatens to undermine the integrity of the self.

Likewise, the workings of an economy of lesbian desire is most often repressed, because this "other way" of desiring cannot be easily appropriated into the hetero-masculine-controlled structures of discourse and representation.[13] It is thus only in the return of repressed bi-textuality that we can begin to read the muted desires of excluded forms of sexuality and subjectivity.

The threat that an exposure of the letter and feminine desire may cause to the subject is demonstrated at the end of the film, when we first see a burning Mrs. Danvers and then the flaming letter *R*. In this instance, the masculine home is being destroyed by a burning desire that materializes itself in the form of an insistent letter. Mrs. Danvers wants to burn down the house, because she now knows that the second Mrs. de Winter has been successfully integrated into the heterosexual-masculine domain.

At the end of *Rebecca*, Manderley, the masculine mansion, has been burnt to the ground along with Mrs. Danvers and all traces of Rebecca's presence. The price that Hitchcock has to pay for the heterosexual containment of bi-textual forces is the destruction of the masculine domain of power and discourse. The heterosexist Symbolic order thus calls for its own destruction by failing to allow for the emergence of multiple forms of sexuality and language.

4

Notorious: Luce Irigaray, Feminine Fluids, and Masculine (Be)Hind-Sight

In the previous chapters, I have discussed some of the reasons why masculine subjects have a fear of both feminine sexuality and unconscious forms of textuality. By encountering multiple modes of identification and desire, Hitchcock's male characters often display a confused sense of self and a loss of linguistic control. In *Notorious*, we shall see how this double horror of the feminine figure and bi-textual desire is linked to the masculine need for solid structures that resist the free flow of feminine desire and bodily secretions. Furthermore, the flowing nature of feminine sexuality and discourse in this film is directly attached to the destabilization of the masculine visual order.

Inverting Masculine Vision

Hitchcock's films have often been used by feminist theorists as examples of the way that men visually control the structure and movement of female bodies. In her book *The Women Who Knew too Much*, Tania Modleski argues that in *Notorious*, the masculine mastery of the visual field is coupled with an attempt to purify the female subject: "After setting the woman up as an object of male desire and curiosity, the film proceeds to submit her to a process of purification whereby she is purged of her excess sexuality in order to be rendered fit for her place in the patriarchal order."[1] Modleski continues by linking this patriarchal process of separating the female subject from her body and her sexuality to the way that men attempt to undermine women's relationship to vision. "Not only does the film disembody the sexual woman, it also continually impairs her vision . . . thus ensuring that man remains in sole control of the gaze—and hence of the knowledge and power with which vision is always associated in the cinema" (61). In this structure, knowledge, power, and vision are all connected to the masculine control over feminine subjectivity.

This insightful reading depends upon the belief that men can actually determine the structure of vision and knowledge. I would like to counter this recurrent theme of masculine mastery in feminist film criticism by closely reading *Notorious* in a visual way. I will argue that most critics have failed to pay attention to the ways that the visual unfolding of Hitchcock's films often challenges and subverts the manifest movement of his plots. One aspect of Hitchcock's bi-textuality is the way that his films use vision and writing in order to counter the claims of verbal discourse. In *Notorious*, the Oedipal movement that places masculine speech and law over feminine subjectivity and sexuality is resisted by the visual insistence of the failure of all forms of representation. More so, this blocking of representation and vision will be directly attached to a censored homoerotic presence in the film.

The very first scene of *Notorious* opens with a view of several male photographers who have their unused cameras placed between their legs. These men cannot employ their phallic cameras because they are placed outside of the closed doors of a courtroom. Therefore, right from the start of the film, men are placed in a position where their visual and representational control of the world is being blocked. This sense of visual impotency is enhanced in this scene by the way that Hitchcock allows the camera to enter the courtroom only at a great distance. In this long-range shot of the court proceedings, we can only see the backs of the lawyer and the man who is being convicted of treason. By not showing the front of these men, Hitchcock not only increases our sense of visual blockage, but he also centers the camera on a rear view of men. In fact, the showing of the backs of men will be one of the recurring images of this film.

This method of not allowing us to see the facial expressions of men not only serves to heighten our sense of visual impotency, but it also indicates a homoerotic relationship between Hitchcock's camera and the male subjects of the film. In the very next scene, where Alicia (Ingrid Bergman) is throwing a party, the camera is blocked by the presence of the back of an unknown male's head. This filmic penetration from behind is coupled with Alicia's attempt to seduce and pick up this mysterious presence. In order to get his attention, she asks: "Haven't I seen you somewhere before?" This question implies that she is the one who is in control of language and vision. This feminine claim to vision and discourse thus challenges the traditional conception of the Hitchcockian female. Alicia is the one who is watching and asking questions, while the silent male figure is denied any level of visual or linguistic control.

What I would like to stress in these opening scenes is the way that Hitchcock employs what Lee Edelman has called "(be)hindsight."[2] Edelman uses this term in order to stress the homoerotic aspects of Freud's theory of the primal scene and the way that Freud always discusses psychological trauma as an event that only becomes traumatic after the fact through a process of hindsight (95). Homosexual encounters thus imply for Freud not only a reversal of sexual positions but also a reversal of temporal relations. Furthermore, Edelman points out that Freud himself insists that children first believe that sexual intercourse takes place from behind (101). In the development of sexual knowledge, this early theory of procreation from behind is replaced by the child through a transformation of sexual positions where the behind becomes the vagina and the parents take on specific gendered roles. "Thus in the first instance the primal scene is always perceived as sodomitical, and it specifically takes shape as a sodomitical scene between sexually undifferentiated parents" (101). Edelman effectively shows in his reading of Freud that the primal scene of sexuality for the subject always entails an element of bisexuality and the penetration from behind.

Due to the fact that this notion of the bisexual primal scene of sodomy reverses many of the heterosexual paradigms of space and temporality, it is continuously being repressed and blocked from representation. However, we know from Freud's theory of the return of the repressed that nothing can be completely negated psychologically, and therefore we can expect an unconscious return of the repressed primal scene. In Hitchcock's films, it is the spectacle of gay male sex that is continuously hinted at but never shown. This failure to show the primal scene results in *Notorious* in the filmic representation of the back of men's bodies, the constant references to castration, the undermining of visual control, and the processes of cross-dressing and cross-identification.

On the manifest level of this film, the narration depicts Alicia's transference of her allegiance away from her convicted German father and towards the American Intelligence agent, Devlin (Cary Grant). This movement is thus structured by the resolution of the Oedipus Complex within a post-World War II international framework. Just as Alicia has to give up her father in order to be with another man, the shift of world power is moved from Germany to America. Yet, Alicia does not complelty resolve this form of Oedipal love in the traditional manner. Instead of identifying with her mother and finding a substitute for her father, she appears to identify with her father. This aspect of Alicia's cross-identification is made apparent after she finds out that her father has killed himself and she tells Devlin: "It is as if something happened to me and not to him. You see, I don't have to hate him anymore." In the logic of this phrase, Alicia is declaring that she has also died along with her father and that her death has allowed her to stop hating herself and her father.

This bi-textual cross-identification between Alicia and her father is further enhanced in one of the following scenes where she is sent to meet and seduce the Nazi, Alex Sebastain. In order to attract this man, Alicia (whose last name is Huber-*man*) dresses up like a man by sporting a tie and jacket. The subtle point of this cross-dressing may be that Alex can only be seduced by a woman masquerading as a man. Furthermore, the portrayal of Alex Sebastian in the film constantly calls to mind references to homosexuality and emasculation. When Alex first sees Devlin's boss, Prescott, who is sitting behind him at a restaurant, he declares to Alicia: "He's rather handsome, isn't he?" This remark will be later repeated by Alicia to Prescott who seems quite pleased by this disclosure. As in many other instances in the film, Alicia serves in this structure as the one who mediates the same-sex desire that is circulated between men.

Doubling this role of female mediation, we find Alex's mother who is the true master of his house. In all of the scenes between Alex and his mother, she is shown as being domineering, while he is depicted as being castrated and impotent. A paradigmatic example of this classic and questionable representation of the controlling mother and the passive (homosexual) son is presented in the scene where Alex has to ask his mother for the key to the house's wine cellar. This cellar is essential to all of the men in the house because it holds the secret to the Nazi's plot. Furthermore, printed on the key is the word "Unica" that points to Alex's eunuch-like status in relation to his mother and his sexuality.

In the first meeting between Alicia and Alex's mother, Alex's emasculation and his mother's dominance is displayed by the mother's constant effort to censor Alex's speech. We can read this act of maternal censoring as the mother's desire to both prevent her son's relationship with another woman and her fear that Alicia cannot be trusted with the family's secrets. The family secret, in turn, can be associated with the primal scene that is blocked from Alicia's and the audience's vision. From this perspective, the McGuffin is not just an empty hole in the middle of Hitchcock's discourse; rather, this missing object (the maternal phallus) takes on a great significance as the sign of the missing primal scene.

In her *Male Subjectivity at the Margins*, Kaja Silverman has effectively outlined the way that the traumatic nature of the primal scene can reduce the viewing male subject to the passive role of the one who knows but cannot act.[3] Her readings of such figures as Henry James coincides with my own concept of bi-textuality by stressing the multiple levels of identification and desire that can be derived from the fundamental fantasy and primal scene. "The primal scene fantasy opens onto both the positive heterosexual and the negative or homosexual versions of the Oedipus Complex . . . it promotes, in other words, desire for the father and identification with the mother, as well as desire for the mother and identification with the father" (165). Since the primal scene occurs for the subject before the recognition of sexual difference, Silverman posits that the initial forms of identification are fundamentally bisexual. In fact, she hints that the child participates in his parents secret copulation as a third party who unconsciously would like to be penetrated by the father from behind while he also penetrates the mother. In this structure, the child presents, "the desire to be sodomized by the "father" while occupying the place of the "mother," and the desire to sodomize him while he is penetrating the 'mother'" (173). Silverman combines both of these cross-gendered forms of desire under the rubric of "sodomitical identification" (174).

In the case of Henry James, this mode of penetration from behind is reflected by this author's constant references to "going behind" his characters and the placement of his narrative voice and eye in the position of a passive onlooker who sees and hears but cannot act (157–158). One reasons for this form of masculine passivity is James' horror of his own sexuality—he knows that his desire is illicit but he cannot help returning to scenes of repressed homosexual desire. Like the child in the primal scene who is forced to watch sexual acts that are outside of his or her control, James places his characters and his narrative voice in a position of visual and representational non-mastery (165).

Silverman directly attaches this lack of control of sexuality and vision to a marginalized from of masculinity that directly counters many claims of feminist film theory: "Here again is voyeurism with a difference, voyeurism which bears no relation to that mastering vision which has been so exhaustively interrogated within film theory" (171). In her criticism of the stress on the masculine mastery of the visual field, Silverman is able to highlight the ways that the knowledge of sexuality most often represents a traumatic de-centering of the masculine subject. "Knowledge leads not to power and social integration, but to loss and isolation" (170).

In *Notorious*, it is precisely this question of knowledge and sexuality that serves to undermine Devlin's and Alicia's vision and control. When Devlin finds out that Alicia has "known" Alex in the past, he becomes enraged and confused. For Devlin, knowledge is directly attached to sexuality and the loss of masculine control. Due to the fact that Alicia has "known" several men, Devlin feels that he cannot trust her and this lack of trust causes him to become irrationally jealous of Alicia's fake relationship with Alex. In the last scene of the film, Devlin's loss of visual control and his sexual jealousy are directly linked together, when he declares: "I couldn't see straight or think straight. I was a fat-headed guy full of pain." Devlin's failure to see or to think in a straight way is therefore a direct result of his jealousy about Alicia's sexual knowledge.

As in Freud's classic formulation of the relationship between homosexuality and paranoia, we can link Devlin's jealousy to his own rejection of same-sex desires. More over, since it is Alicia whose vision has been rendered confused and distorted throughout the film, Devlin's declaration of his inability to see straight can be directly associated to his identification with Alicia's own visual impairment. As the passive male subject whose masculinity is constantly being called into question, Devlin's identification with Alicia places him in a passive position in relation to Alicia's own active and masculinized identification. In other words, the repressed homosexuality of this film's unseen primal scene is centered on a sexual relationship where the gendered roles of the masculine and feminine subjects are reversed. On this level of bi-textuality, it is Hitchcock's camera itself that cannot see straight as it penetrates from behind.

Feminine Fluids, Masculine Forms

In order to further explore this disruption of the masculine control of vision, I would like to discuss Luce Irigary's theory of feminine fluidity. In her book *The Sex Which Is Not One*, Irigaray argues that feminine sexuality is characterized by a flow of fluids that is incompatible with the structures and forms of most of our systems of representation:

Now if we examine the properties of fluids, we note that this "real" may well include, and in large measure, a physical reality that continues to resist adequate symbolization and/or signifies the powerlessness of logic to incorporate in its writing the characteristic features of nature.[4]

In the binary logic of this passage, Irigaray insists that femininity, fluids, the Real, and nature resist the logic of symbolization and reason.[5] This focus on the collusion between the Symbolic order and the mechanics of solids offers a new twist to the old debate between masculine form and feminine matter. For it is no longer just a question of women being equated with the Real, due to their abjected status within the Symbolic order, but now the problem or trouble has moved to the very notion of materiality and the Real itself. We must ask with Irigaray, in what way are our conceptions of matter and form based on a concentration of solid material that precludes any acknowledgement of material that is fluid and transforming?

Irigaray affirms that feminine discourse and existence must be thought of in other terms than in the mechanics of solids. She posits that femininity is "continuous, compressible, dilatable, viscous, conductible, diffusible. . . . That it is unending, potent, and impotent owing to its resistance to the countable . . . it is already diffuse 'in itself,' which disconcerts any attempt at static identification" (11). The resistance of the feminine for Irigaray is thus a resistance that is due to the viscous and flowing nature of feminine existence. But is this existence defined by the purely biological categories of sexual secretion and lactation or is Irigaray pointing to a non-biological notion of fluidity?

It would seem that, in fact, Irigaray bases her notion of feminine fluids not on an extended biological metaphor, but rather on an analysis of feminine discourse. "And yet that woman-thing speaks. But not 'like,' 'the same,' not 'identical with itself' nor to any x, etc. Not a 'subject,' unless transformed by phallocratism. It speaks 'fluid'" (11). From this perspective, the flow of feminine discourse is due to the fluctuating and contradictory quality of a speech that has to mime the words of the Other, yet constitutes its presence in-between the lines and outside of them.

In turning now to *Notorious*, we find an excellent elaboration of this dialectic between feminine flow and masculine form. Starting with the second scene of this film, Hitchcock consistently associates Alicia with liquids and the upsetting of the visual and narrative field. She and alcohol are virtually inseparable; we watch her drink and offer drinks to others, we watch Devlin command her to drink an ambiguous anti-hangover concoction, and we watch twice as she drinks poisoned coffee.

In two scenes where male American agents are discussing Alicia, her alcohol consumption is a transparent euphemism for her sexual promiscuity. Devlin also engages in this connection, when he says to her, "You've been sober for eight days, and as far as I can tell, you've made no new conquests." By linking her drinking to her sexuality, we see why she poses a threat to her male counterparts. She is the fluid nature of the Real that cannot be counted on or controlled by their discourse or modes of representation.

In order to contain this threat of fluidity, the men in the film are constantly trying to cover her and bottle her up—all of these men want to interiorize and internalize her feminine flow. Furthermore, the major tool for these acts of control in the film are the bottles of wine that contain in themselves a special liquid that can either destroy or render people intoxicated.

These bottles of wine play a complicated bi-textual function in the film; they serve as both Symbolic phallic signifiers and as potentially open vaginal containers. On the phallic level, the person who possesses the bottles also possesses Alicia and believes that he or she controls the Symbolic order of power and discourse. On the vaginal level, the bottles are containers of a dangerous fluidity, which once open are able to spread out and threaten the stability of the masculine world.

In an early reference to this connection between feminine fluidity and the possibility of structural destruction, Alicia, while pouring Devlin a drink, states, "I am a marked woman. I'm liable to blow up the Panama Canal at any minute now." The canal is precisely a structure that is made in order to control and direct the flow of water. Thus, by saying that she could blow it up, Alicia is highlighting the way that her fluid nature stands as a threat to men.

The possibility that Devlin is menaced by her femininity comes out in the open when he confesses, "I've always been scared of women." Her response is to say that in reality he is afraid of himself, afraid of the fact that he is in love with her. Alicia's reply points to the fact that Devlin's problem with women is connected to the way that he views himself. In other words, this masculine subject does not want to fall in love because he fears that love will cause him to be feminized. This fear of feminization is given credence, when Devlin replies to Alicia's claim that he is in love, by stating: "that wouldn't be hard." The triple meaning of the word "hard" in this passage cannot go unnoticed. On the most obvious level, Devlin is agreeing that Alicia would be easy to fall in love with. On another level, he points to his impotency and the fact that he is afraid of women. Finally, the opposition to hardness points to the threat of fluidity that menaces his own masculinity.

We can consider that the flow of the feminine is the excluded center of masculinity; this fluidity must be contained and controlled in order to maintain the rigid structures of law and language.[6] The political dimension to the masculine containment of Alicia's fluidity is introduced in the opening scene when her father is sentenced for being a spy. At the end of his trial, we hear Alicia's father threaten the judge by exclaiming "You can put me away, but you can't put away what is going to happen to you and the whole country." Once again the theme here is the social attempt of containing something in order to stop it from spreading and flowing. More so, when we first see Alicia, we hear the police telling her that she better not leave town, and in this way, the control of her movements is linked to the control of her father.

After her father's trial, Alicia exits from the court, and she is surrounded by photographers who shout out, "Hold it Miss Huberman." Once again, all of the male figures want her to remain still so they can en-frame her in their pictures and forms of representation. We can read this call for framing as Hitchcock's own awareness of his need to frame and direct women in his films. The upsetting flow of femininity is thus constantly posed as being both a threat to the masculine controlled world of political representation, as well as the foundations and contents of the male structure itself.

In order to counter this claim for fixation of movement and the stability of forms, Alicia begins to drink and drink. She decides that she wants to take Devlin for a ride, but because of her intoxicated state, she is unable to steer straight. The audience cannot but help to be fearful for the couple due to her dangerous driving that her consumption of liquids has caused. At one point, as we watch the camera swerve and dip with the car, she complains that she cannot see because of the fog, while in fact, the problem is that her own hair is in her eyes. The loss of control of vision and the stable frame of the camera is thus connected to not only her consumption of liquids, but also to the flowing of her feminine hair.

By linking intoxication to femininity, Hitchcock is able to expose one of the unconscious fears that masculine subjects have in regard to the female flow. The liquid nature of her movements and discourse place the feminine subject in a position to resist and undermine the masculine drive for contained order and fixed forms of representation. It is well-known that male subjects often feel that they have to repress their emotions and hold back their tears precisely to avoid being overwhelmed with a form of existence that they do not think they can master. At one point in the film, when Alicia starts to cry, the cold Devlin states, "Dry your eyes, baby; it's out of character." This flow that is externalized from the female character has to be forced back in by the male subject. Once again here, the term "character" has a triple reference that can point to Alicia's personality, Bergman's role, and the integrity of the letter. In order to be a good spy, Alicia cannot show any true emotion. Likewise, in order to be a good actress, Bergman has to remember what her role is, and more radically, in order to be a good figure of representation, the female subject must not allow for too much externalization of her feminine nature. The central threat that femininity poses for the masculine subject is thus the potential that this fluid nature may upset the different modes of discourse and representation that are fundamental to the masculine sense of self.

In the morning that follows Alicia's drunk driving, Hitchcock links together the themes of feminine fluids, masculine law, and the upsetting of the visual field. When Alicia wakes up, the camera focuses on a drink that is sitting in front of her. We then see Devlin's darkened image from a slanted angle and we hear him sternly say to her, "You better drink it. Go on drink it." This will not be the only time in the film that we will watch Alicia be force-fed a liquid from a male figure. Instead of her choosing what and when she wants to drink, she now has become subjected to the regulation of fluids by the Other. This regulation is made necessary because of the way that she continues to threaten the field of representation.

While we watch her lay on the bed, the camera takes on her subjective camera angle and we see the image of Devlin slowly get turned upside down. She then asks him, "What's your angle?" The double meaning of this phrase points to the fact that he is trying to pursue some agenda with her and to the angle of the camera itself. It is as if she is laying on the bed, talking to Hitchcock himself and asking him from what angle is he taking the shot. This blending of the camera angle with her own part in Devlin's plot is reinforced when she responds to Devlin's request that he help her with, "So you can frame me." Thus, Alicia/Bergman is well aware of the way that the director or male agent is attempting to put a border on her that will turn her into a stable form of representation.

Modleski argues that the impairment of Alicia's vision in this scene is an example of the way that she is punished for her "notorious" sexual reputation (61). While, I would not disagree with this argument, I would like to radicalize it by insisting that when women do get hold of the visual field, they at times actively challenge it and submit it to their flow. Therefore, just as women may work to subvert the realm of language by citing and displacing the words and codes of the Other, they may also have a similar effect on a visual level.[7]

However, even if we posit the radical nature of Alicia's destabilizing of the visual field, we must still consider that the dominant movement of the film is to control and internalize her dangerous flow. When she does agree to her mission with the federal agents, we find out that she is needed because she has had a love affair with Alex in the past. In one scene, we see a meeting of agents who insist that they have to have someone "inside" the house and inside Sebastian's confidence. In other words, the men need to mobilize Alicia's flow inside another masculine domain.

We must remember that the FBI are not alone in their efforts to contain Alicia and her fluidity. Almost every man Alicia encounters attempts this sort of physical control. In the first scene, her father's sailing friend wants to carry her off in a boat. Then when Devlin first meets her, one of his first actions is to cover her first with a jacket and then with a scarf that he ties around her exposed stomach. Later, Alex will try to contain her in his house and prevent her from leaving.

Even Alicia's attire throughout the film emphasizes the entrapment of the female figure within the masculine structure. In the first party scene, she wears a short blouse, which has black and white bars running across it. Then, in a later party scene at Sebastian's house, she wears a dress that is cut so a diamond frame encircles her neck. This diamond shape is then doubled by the pattern on the floor that looks much like a chessboard.[8] Furthermore, in this scene, the belt encircling her waist is no longer a concealing scarf, instead, it is now a jeweled link chain. From the scarf to the chain, she has moved from a position of being merely covered to one of being imprisoned.

This entrapment of the female figure in the film is doubled by the relation between bottles and the possession of Alicia's allegiance. At the beginning of her love affair with Devlin, Alicia requests that he bring her a bottle of wine. He does go out and buy her a bottle of champagne, but he leaves it at the U.S. embassy when he finds out that Alicia is going to rekindle a relationship with Sebastian in order to spy on him. We next see Alicia having wine when she is in Sebastian's house. The movement of the wine and champagne follows the movement of Alicia and the men that try to control her. From her own home, to an apartment with Devlin, to the Embassy to Sebastian's house, she is surely the object of exchange that circulates among the different power structures of the film.[9] Furthermore, as a representative of liquidity, Alicia can be, in part equated with the secret wine that everyone in Sebastian's house is making such a big fuss over. Her investigation of this fluid is, in this sense, an investigation into her own feminine fluidity. However, her access to this hidden and secretive liquid is blocked, because she does not have the key to the wine cellar.[10]

The movement of this key also determines a pathway of power circulation in the film. At first Sebastian's mother has the key, and she appears to be the one who is in charge and dominates her son. Then we see that Sebastian has it himself, but Alicia soon steals it from him and gives it to Devlin. Paradoxically, the "Unica" key is both a symbol of Symbolic control and one of threatened emasculation. As in Poe's famous story of the "Purloined Letter," whoever has the key or letter is forced into a position of inaction.[11] In order for the key to retain its power, it cannot be used or revealed.

When Alex Sebastian's mother has the phallus-key, Alex himself is shown to be emasculated. He has no access to the doors and the hidden rooms of his own house. Then, when Alicia takes it from him, he becomes castrated once again and now his castration could cause his death. In the final scene of the film, Sebastian's emasculation is highlighted by the fact that he cannot act to defend his interests, nor can he even speak. If he tries to stop Devlin and Alicia from leaving his home, he will expose to his fellow Nazis that he has married a spy and thus they will kill him. At this point in the film, Alex is placed in the position of the masochistic male subject who is forced to watch the primal scene but cannot participate in it.

Linked to this emasculation of the marginalized male subject, we find Alicia's attempt to gain control over the circulation of fluids at the bottom of the house. This reversal of gender roles begins when Alicia and Devlin sneak into Alex's wine cellar. At first, Alicia appears from deep within the interior, while Devlin is pacing outside of it. This positioning of Devlin outside and Alicia inside serves to accentuate Alicia's imprisoned situation. This is further emphasized by the fact that when she approaches Devlin, jail-like shadows bar her body.

Since Devlin and Alicia suspect that something is hidden within the wine bottles, Devlin begins to examine them and he accidently knocks one over. Instead of wine pouring out of the broken bottle, what looks to be black sand spills out on the floor. Here, we have an interesting transition, because the feminine fluidity has now been transformed into the materiality of a solid substance. Furthermore, what first anticipates this transition is the way that the phallic bottle falls and crashes to the ground. If we read this broken bottle as a sign of castration, we can also read the solid insides as a materialization of the feminine flow that now begins to resist the masculine structure. Instead of the feminine subject having her flowing nature contained in masculine forms, we now have a feminine solid that spills out of a broken male structure.

This reversal is continued in the scene when we see Devlin attempt to hide the fact that the phallic bottle has been broken, by putting its cork back in. This movement reverses the usual orgasmic popping of the masculine bottle. Instead of foamy liquid shooting out of the phallic bottle, we now have a cork placed in the center of the vaginal hole. The film therefore begins to present a reversal of the dialectic between the masculine container and the feminine flow. Alicia has managed to undermine the power structure by stealing the phallic key from the master of the house.

Another indication of this structural reversal is the scene that immediately precedes the action in the wine cellar. While Alicia and Devlin are waiting to escape down to the cellar, they become afraid that the bartender may run out of champagne and then he will have to ask Alex for the missing key to fetch more alcohol. In order to add an element of suspense, the camera watches the steady removal of upright champagne bottles from their bucket. With each removal of a bottle, Alicia and Devlin realize that they are getting closer to being caught. But what do these upright bottles symbolize if not the phallus itself? And if we are watching the removal of the phallic bottles, isn't the anxiety that we experience precisely an anxiety of the menace of castration? The key being called "Unica" thus make sense, because the symbol of phallic power and control is being constantly threatened in the film.

When, Alex finally gets his key back and he goes down to discover what is going on with the wine cellar, he first sees a liquid stain in the sink, then he sees that one of the bottles has the wrong date, and finally he sees some ore on the ground. The liquid stain is a residue of the feminine fluid, which in turn, has caused a disruption of the Symbolic order (the wrong date on the bottle) and has now left a hard material trace (the ore). The original Real liquid has been transformed into a material rem(a)inder or what Lacan would call the "object (a)" that now disrupts the Symbolic system. Feminine fluidity is thus transformed into the mechanics of solids, once that liquid has passed through the Symbolic order. However, the discovery of this process serves to reverse its entire order. Since, Alicia has discovered the key to the manipulation and transformation of her own feminine flow, she must in some way cause the system to regress so that the material objects and forms are transformed back into flowing liquids.

Re-Circulation of the Feminine Flow

Once Sebastian realizes that Alicia is a spy, he goes to his mother's bedroom in order to ask for her advice. Here, the power structure of the house shifts back to the mother's control. She tells Sebastian that Alicia "must be allowed to move about freely, but she will be on a leash. She will have nothing further to inform." The mother reasons that since they cannot completely control Alicia, they must attempt to regulate her flow and to prevent her from taking a form (informing). They will attempt to accomplish this task by poisoning her slowly. Although, in order to do this, they must force her to drink and thus they actively participate in the recirculation of the feminine fluids. At this point in the film, the movement is no longer to contain her flow within the house, but to allow her flow to externalize itself.

The externalization of the internalized female figure, thus, potentially represents a reversal of the masculine discourse on feminine sexuality. Alicia must be allowed to leave the mansion, because her flow can no longer be contained within the power structure of the film. Furthermore, her exit from Sebastian's house leaves all of the men in the film immobilized, except Devlin who cannot see or think straight.

This "feminization" of the men in the film through the materialization of the feminine subject points to a new possibility of political resistance and transformation. If women take hold of their own material representation, they may be able to render their own flow more solid, while they allow rigid masculine structures to become more fluid. This would also entail a privileging of scattered contents over the solidification of hardened containers and forms of representation.

Notorious reworks the themes of sexual ambiguity and textual multiplicity and presents them on a visual level. The blocked vision of the primal scene and the flowing disruption of the visual field in this film both contribute to a masculine sense of Imaginary impotency. However, the effects of this realization of visual non-mastery is often contradictory. From one perspective, the menace of losing control over vision and language may cause subjects to seek out more oppressive and obvious forms of mastery. This is shown when Devlin reacts to Alicia's drunk driving and verbal resistance by physically knocking her out. On the other hand, the disruption of visual control can allow for the emergence of multiple forms of desire and identification. In Hitchcock's case, the constant threat of the emergence of destabilizing modes of sexuality results in a displaced homo-eroticization of the camera that can only penetrate its subjects from behind.

5

Vertigo: Sexual Dis-Orientation and the En-gendering of the Real

In my reading of *Notorious*, I stressed the different ways that the masculine control of vision and language is under-mined by the presence of bi-textual desires and identifica-tions. This focus on the failures of masculine mastery contradicts many of the claims of recent feminist film theory that depend on the binary opposition between masculine visual control and the objectified female body. I have not tried to deny that men attempt to visually master females; rather, I have shown how many of these attempts at control often fail. Furthermore, the failure to master the representation of the female subject has been shown to present a form of mas-culine loss that motivates the male subject to find new ways to convert lack into a form of representational plentitude.

In *Vertigo*, one witnesses a constant alternation between the attempt to control and shape the feminine form on the one hand, and on the other hand, a deep awareness of mascu-line loss and lack. On a manifest level, this film depicts the diverse ways that a woman is subjected to the Symbolic con-struction of gender. The character of Judy Barton (Kim Novak) has been hired to pretend that she is a wealthy man's wife. In the structure of the story, this substitute female must perform and reiterate a prescripted feminine role.

From a certain perspective, we can say that Judy Barton is a female impersonator who not only points to the constructed nature of all gender performances, but also allows us to see how sexual difference is determined by the Symbolic death drive. As a subject who is playing the role of someone that is possessed by the dead spirit of another woman, this character represents the vanishing and return of the female subject in the signifying chain. Slavoj Zizek has interpreted this process in the following terms: "If the false Madeline resembles herself, it is because she is in a way already dead. The hero loves her as Madeline in so far as she is dead—the sublimation of her figure is equivalent to her mortification in the real."[1] Due to the fact that Judy is only a Symbolic representation of Madeline, she has no life of her own and therefore she can be considered to be already dead. However, Judy's submission to this Symbolic mandate is never complete and it is her resistance to this process of representation that I would like to focus on.

As Zizek points out, the film itself can be divided into two halves that repeat the same story but with a crucial difference (83–87). In the first half of the film, we watch Judy seduce Scottie (James Stewart) by following Gavin Elster's orders and pretending to be Madeline possessed by her Great-grandmother Carlotta Valdez. In the second half of the film, Scottie encounters Judy Barton and he himself tries to turn her into Madeline. Thus, both main men in the film try to transform the Real Judy into a Symbolic substitute. Elster wishes to make this substitution because he wishes to kill his real wife, while Scottie desires to subject Judy to this performance in order to re-find his lost love-object. In both of these cases, men seek to control and master the performance and construction of femininity.

If Judy Barton never returned in the second half of the film, we could say that *Vertigo* does indeed represent the subjection of women to the masculine control of vision and language. However, her return within the structure of the film points to the impossibility to completely repress and efface the female subject. Like Hitchcock himself, who cannot stop showing up in his own films, Judy's returning presence points to the resistance of the female form to all acts of Symbolic disembodiment. Furthermore, this resistance of the female subject is directly attached to the way that she reverses the "normal" structure of film vision.

Marian Keane has argued in an article entitled, "A Closer Look at Scopophilia: Mulvey, Hitchcock and *Vertigo*," that the turning point of *Vertigo* occurs when Judy looks directly at the camera for the first time.[2] When this female figure stares back at the camera, the viewers and Hitchcock, the director, are now the object of another's gaze and unknowable desire. In this structural reversal, the female object becomes a looking subject who undermines the very basis of film representation. I would like to read Judy Barton's look as an indication of Hitchcock's own desire to resist completely killing off and effacing the original Real Thing. By having the feminine object look at us, we no longer remain comfortable being the one that watches and represents the Other.

In the opening credits of the film, we first see an image of a woman's eye that looks towards the audience. This staring female gaze represents an inversion of the image of the back of a man's head that dominates *Notorious*. We can read this reversal as an indication of Hitchcock's bi-textuality. On the most manifest level of the film, the story does depict the ways that men attempt to visually master females but on a more latent and visual level, we witness the dominance of female vision and the presence of masculine loss.

The main way that this sense of masculine lack and loss of visual control is demonstrated in the film is through Scottie's fear of heights. In the opening scene, Scottie is attempting to chase a man over a series of rooftops but as soon as he looks down to the ground, he becomes anxious and his vision becomes distorted. His anxiety is therefore linked to his loss of control over his own vision and his ability to control his movements. In the second scene of the film, his horror of the deep abyss becomes directly attached to a horror of femininity and his fear of falling in love with the mother-substitute, Midge.

Throughout the opening scenes, Midge is directly attached to the role of maternal love for Scottie. When she tries to convince him not to rejoin the police force, Scottie responds: "Midge don't be so motherly."Following this remark, Scottie switches the subject and asks her about the bra that she is designing. She replies to this question concerning female undergarments in the following manner: "It's a brassiere, you know about those things, you're a big boy now."The effect of this statement is to point out Scottie's child-like status in relation to the motherly Midge and the question of feminine sexuality.

Doubling Midge's maternalization, we find Scottie's "feminization."In one of the first lines of the film, Scottie complains that the corset that he is wearing is too tight. He then asks Midge if she thinks that many men wear corsets, her response is: "More than you think." The irony of this encounter is heightened by the fact that while Scottie is complaining about the tightness of this female article, Midge is actively designing another female undergarment. This reverses the traditional structure where men design and women wear.

After the feminization of Scottie and the maternalization of Midge have been established in this scene, Scottie attempts to get over his fear of heights by climbing on top of a chair. While he climbs up, Midge is placed beneath him. At one point, he looks down and he becomes anxious again. Due to his sense of anxiety, he appears to faint and fall into the arms of Midge. I would like to read Midge's position below the falling Scottie as equivalent to the open spaces that make him anxious. In other words, Scottie's fear of heights is also a fear of femininity.

In order to explain this connection between masculine anxiety and feminine presence, I will turn towards Lacan's discussion of Freud's famous dream of "Irma's Injection."[3] Lacan argues that when Freud looks into the mouth of his female patient, he associates this open organ with the female genitalia:

> There's a tremendous discovery here, that of the flesh one never sees, the foundation of things, the other side of the head, of the face, the secretory glands par excellence, the flesh from which everything exudes, at the very heart of the mystery, the flesh in as much as it is suffering, is formless, in as much as its form in itself is something which provokes anxiety. (154)

What causes the anxiety of the male subject is precisely this encounter with a formless form, for if the other has no unified image or body, then the subject's own body is called into question. Lacan points to this connection between the form of Freud's patient and Freud's experience of his own body, when he continues his discussion by adding that this "spectre of anxiety" produces a revelation that says to the looking male subject: "You are this, which is so far from you, this which is the ultimate formlessness" (155). The male subject's horror of the female sexual organ is in this instance a horror of the subject's own sense of nothingness.

I would like to argue that in Lacan's theory of castration anxiety, the male subject is not primarily afraid of recognizing the female's genitals because they represent the possibility that he can lose his own genitals or phallus, but rather because he is afraid of seeing in the other, a reflection of his own nothingness. The encounter with the feminine object, then, serves to undermine the ego's sense of bodily unity and coherency. Since the ego of consciousness defines itself completely by the image of the other, and if the other's image is found to be lacking, the subject experiences his or her own self as a lack.[4]

However, the terms "lack" and "nothingness" are ultimately misleading here because what Lacan really wants to say is that these forms of absence represent the presence of a Real that resists being Symbolized or Imagined:[5]

> Hence there's an anxiety provoking apparition of an image which summarizes what we can call the revelation of that which is least penetrable in the real, of the real lacking any possible mediation, of the ultimate real, of the essential object which isn't an object any longer, but something faced with which all words cease and all categories fail, the object of anxiety par excellence (164)

In this passage, the feminine object is placed in a position to be outside the Symbolic order of words, categories, and mediation. By equating the female form with the Real that cannot be symbolized, Lacan places this female subject in a position of unknowability. However, I would like to affirm that, if we maintain Freud's theory of foundational bi-sexuality, the horror of the Real is fundamentally a horror of the lack of sexual orientation.

Lee Edelman has connected this confusion that is caused by the presence of sexual dis-orientation to the structure of a moebious strip: "Now what distinguishes the moebious strip, of course, is the impossibility of distinguishing its front from its back, a condition that has . . . immediate sexual resonance; but that indistinguishibility bespeaks as well a crisis of certainty, a destabilizing of the foundational logic of which knowledge itself as such depends."[6] Edelman argues that in the child's viewing of the primal scene, there is a confusion between the front and the back of the mother as the target of sexual penetration. Furthermore, if the primal scene of sexuality takes place in a period prior to the discovery of sexual difference, the original object of the subject's sexual vision is a bi-sexual organ that marks a continuity between masculinity and femininity. This original sexual object represents a structure where all differences are collapsed and the opposite ends of the sexual spectrum are attached in a moebious-like structure.

The presence of this type of de-stabilizing topological figure occurs throughout *Vertigo*. In the opening credits,we see a series of shapes that emerge from the female eye that stares at the audience. One of the first figures that is produced from this feminine look is a moebious strip. Later on in the film, we will find the same figure in the form of Madeline's and Carlotta's hairstyles. This figure represents a surface that turns in on itself and makes a certain presence absent as well as an absence present.[7]

In his discussion of the fundamental relationship between the subject and the Real Thing in his *Ethics of Psychoanalysis* seminar, Lacan uses this same structure of the moebious strip: "In reality Das Ding has to be posited as exterior, as the prehistoric Other that is impossible to forget . . . something strange to me, although it is at the heart of me, something that on the level of the unconscious only a representation can represent."[8] Here, Lacan articulates a spacial figure that is defined by its center being exterior to itself. In the case of a moebius strip, this is possible because there is a continuous movement from the inside of the structure to the outside. For Lacan, the subject of the unconscious is determined by this form, where the external discourse of the Other becomes the internal desire of the subject. Lacan's schema *L* is itself later articulated as a moebius strip, because the center of the structure is designed to represent an overlapping surface with its opposite ends being tied together.[9]

The moebious strip appears to be a bi-textual figure; yet, the encounter with this dis-orienting object most often becomes associated in Lacan's discourse with the presence of feminine sexuality. This transformation of the bisexual object to a feminized form occurs through the equation of the original Thing with the mother:

> What we find in the incest law is located as such at the level of the unconscious in relation to Das Ding, the Thing. The desire for the mother cannot be satisfied. . . . The function of the pleasure principle is to make man always search for what he has to find again, but which he never will attain.[10]

It is obvious from this passage, that Lacan determines the original object for every subject to be the mother and not a bisexual object located prior to the discovery of sexual difference.

By transforming the original Thing into the mother, Lacan and Freud participate in a cultural disavowal of bisexuality and a reinforcement of the myth that equates femininity with nature. This entails that one of the unseen consequences of equating the Oedipus Complex with the structure of language is that women become associated retroactively with the natural realm of bi-textual confusion. In this sense, the horror of the feminine represents a displaced horror of bisexuality.

Sublimation and Melancholia

In his *Ethics* seminar, Lacan discusses the central ways that the dominant cultural order uses to cultivate and hide the anxiety-provoking Thing or object. In order to encounter this object that causes one to desire, without producing a state of anxiety, the subject has to find a way of reintroducing the object into either the Imaginary and Symbolic orders. In *Vertigo*, there are several forms of sublimation that are represented. One strategy that a subject can employ is to transform the other into a Symbolic symptom or to submit the other to the Symbolic death drive of representation. Another tactic is to idealize the image of the object so that it takes on an Imaginary form.[11] Of course all of these strategies seem to involve the way that men deal with the feminine object and not the other way around.

In fact, it has been pointed out that the history of sublimation and Symbolic representation has been controlled by the masculine attempt to create ideal forms and images out of the raw material of the feminine object.[12] In her early essay entitled "The Dread of Women," Karen Horney states, "May not this be one of the principle roots of the whole masculine impulse to creative work—the never-ending conflict between the man's longing for the woman and his dread of her?"[13] In other words, what pushes men to be creative is their simultaneous fear of and attraction to women. By attempting to form the female object, men are able to keep this potentially engulfing object at a distance."The attitude of love and adoration signifies: 'There is no need to dread a being so wonderful, so beautiful, nay so saintly'" (136). We will see that the central theme of *Vertigo* is precisely Scottie's attempt to keep his love-object on this level of beauty and wonder, in order to hide her true "dreadful" presence.

One of the ways that a masculine subject can attempt to sublimate his relationship with his original love-object is by placing his beloved in the position of an Imaginary identification. Throughout the first part of the film, we watch as Madeline mirrors the figure and form of Carlotta. In one scene, she sits in front of a painting of Carlotta as if she is sitting in front of a mirror. Scottie, who is spying on her from behind, notices that she has the same hair-style and flowers as her dead ancestor. This mirroring relationship has been set-up by Madeline's husband who wants to convince Scottie that *Made*line is actually "mad" like her Great-grandmother.

Since Gavin controls Madeline's mirroring of another woman, Hitchcock is able to show how the feminine Imaginary order is itself dictated by masculine forces.

Furthermore, Madeline/Judy offers herself an explanation of why women might gravitate to this predetermined mirroring structure. In pretending to be in a trance, Madeline/Judy tells Scottie that she often dreams the same thing: "It's as if I'm walking down a long corridor that once was mirrored and fragments of that mirror still hang there. And when I come to the end of that corridor, there's nothing but darkness, and I know that when I walk into the darkness that I will die." Madeline/Judy realizes in her dream that there is only darkness and nothingness outside of the world of mirroring images. As a female subject whose form has been shaped by a man (Gavin Elster), Judy/Madeline is nothing but the construction of the Other. Outside of this construction there is only an unknown terrain of horror, death, and darkness.

Linked to Madeline's/Judy's mirroring of Carlotta, we also find Midge's attempt to paint herself into Scottie's desire. Since she is jealous of Scottie's attention, Midge copies the painting of Carlotta that is found in the art museum. She does a very accurate rendition of this picture, but she replaces Carlotta's face with her own. On seeing this replacement, Scottie reacts with a sense of disgust. We can attribute his reaction to the fact that Midge represents a maternal figure who is supposed to be effaced by his fantasy love-object. By placing her own face in the center of this Imaginary structure, Midge subverts this process of erasing all traces of the original maternal object. As Freud points out in his essay "On the Universal Tendency to Debasement in the Sphere of Love," if the male subject thinks that his beloved is too much like his mother, he will become impotent because of the guilt he feels over the incest taboo.[14] Furthermore, in Freud's theory, the only way to overcome this guilt is for the male subject to split his love life between the pursuance of an all-loving maternal object and an object of pure desire and lust.

If Midge plays the role of the symptomatic love-object, it is Madeline who becomes the object of pure desire. Scottie is able to overcome his dread of the female and his guilt over the mother-substitute by finding a love-object who represents in herself the death of the mother and the transformation of the feminine object into a purely Symbolic presence.[15] Furthermore, in transforming the female form from being an object of dread to being an object of the dead, the male subject is able to perform the essential act of sublimation that Lacan defines as raising an object to the dignity of the Thing.[16]

In his seminar on *Ethics*, Lacan has not yet fully developed his theory of the object (*a*) and so The Thing at times seems to waver between being the pure Real thing-in-itself (the Real before the Symbolic order) and being a rem(a)inder of the Real. While at times this Thing is considered to be the first Other or the mother (52, 71, 106), at other times it serves to represent the presence of the mother as already lost (68–70). This dialectic of two different forms of The Thing, follows Slavoj Zizek's discussion in *The Sublime Object of Ideology* of the two different forms of the Real in Lacan's work:

> We have the real as the starting point, the basis, the foundation of the process of symbolization . . . that is the real which in a sense precedes the symbolic order. . . . But the real is at the same time the product, remainder, leftover, scraps of this process of symbolization. (169).

These two opposing ways of defining the Real respond to the difference between the original Thing that is impossible to symbolize and the object (*a*) that is an excluded element produced by the Symbolic order. If in the act of sublimation, the subject raises an object to the dignity of the Thing, this could mean that the creative act involves the attempt to return to the lost state of the Real Thing before the imposition of the Symbolic order. This however would seem to entail a paradox, because if the Real is really impossible to Symbolize, how can one ever hope to represent it?

Lacan's response to this is to argue that sublimation concerns the making of the absence or void of the original Thing present (130). Thus, the artist doesn't just make a Real thing re-appear, but rather the artist shows the hole or void that has been left behind in the process of trying to Symbolize the Real. Lacan turns to Heidegger's discussion of the vase in his text on *Das Ding*, to argue that this form "creates the void and thereby introduces the possibility of filling it" (120). By stressing the creation of the void and the initial emptiness of the vase, Lacan seeks to emphasize the fact that the art object makes the absence of the Thing appear.

One way that absence is materialized in art is through the presentation of a failure of representation."The Thing is characterized by the fact that it is impossible for us to imagine it. The problem of sublimation is located on this level" (125). In fact, concerning the art object, Lacan will point out the way that certain artists highlight the artificialness of their own work: "What we seek in the illusion is something in which the illusion as such in some way transcends itself, destroys itself, by demonstrating that it is only there as a signifier" (136). In Hitchcock's work we find constant references to this artificial nature of representation and the artist's desire to go beyond the realm of the representation and touch the Real by calling into question the status of the art object itself.

Of course, Lacan's entire argument about the nature of artistic sublimation can be applied to an analysis of the masculine shaping of the female form. In other words, it is not only the artist who seeks to make the absence of the Thing present, but it is also the lover, who seeks to locate the void in his beloved. Lacan himself makes this connection by turning to the tradition of Courtly Love, where the praise of the woman serves to efface her very existence."She is essentially identified with a social function that leaves no room for her person or her own liberty" (147). The Lady in the tradition of Courtly Love is a pure object of exchange who represents an ideal form of love, which is defined by her inaccessibility (149). Moreover, "the Lady" of the song and the poem must be one who is separated by a certain barrier, and it is this barrier that materializes the social taboo against incest.[17]

By rendering the Lady unattainable through the poetry of Courtly Love, Lacan argues that "it was possible to give an object, which in this case is called the Lady, the value of representing the Thing" (126). In other words, Lacan insists that in her inaccessibility, the woman makes the incest taboo even more apparent, and in this way she serves a purely social function. Yet, at the same time, the more that "The Lady" embodies this taboo, the more she becomes a cause of the subject's desire.

One of the functions of sublimation and Courtly Love is thus the transformation of the original bisexual Thing into a heterosexual object-choice. The female subject in the structure of masculine desire becomes the embodiment of the absence of the mother and the proof of the power of men to turn the bi-textual Real into a Symbolic representation of sexual difference. In *Vertigo*, it is clear that Gavin Elster is the one who controls the signifying chain and helps to determine what Scottie's desire will be by manipulating what the different feminine objects will represent.

When we first view Mr. Elster at his office, we see behind him a large glass window that looks out onto his impressive shipbuilding yard. He is a master builder, who is continuously associated with "power," "money," and "freedom."[18] As a productive force, he is able to create out of nothing and to create nothingness itself.[19] For the way that he is able to use the false Madeline to seduce Scottie is by constantly connecting her to the presence of absence.

In the opening section of the film, there is a marked contrast between the scenes with Midge and Mr. Elster and the scenes with Madeline. In the male-oriented scenes, there is a dominance of straight lines, pillars and posts, while in Madeline's scenes there is a consistent use of arches. In this Freudian topography that runs throughout Hitchcock's work, pillars represent phallic lines, while arches curve around the presence of the absent object.

When Madeline first goes to the church to see Carlotta's grave, we see a series of arch-shaped figures: the curved back window of Scottie's car, the archway of the church, the arched doorway, and the arch tombstones. All of these arched structures serve to make the absence of the Thing present. In fact, Lacan argues in his *Ethics* seminar that religion functions by respecting the "emptiness" of the absent Thing (130). In other words, the spaciousness of the church makes God's absence more present and because we are haunted by this absence, we are induced to fill it with our religious beliefs. Likewise, the tombstone itself points to the absence of a being that is rendered present through its Symbolization.

After Madeline leaves this church and graveyard, she goes to a museum where she stares at a painting of the already dead Carlotta Valdez. Like the church, the architecture of the museum is dominated by arches and curved surfaces. Once again, these structures make present the constitutive emptiness that Lacan attaches to all forms of art (130). This presence of the void is accented by the hairstyle that Madeline and the painted Carlotta both wear. These female forms embody a movement around a central lack. Thus, there is a homology between the church, the art museum and Carlotta/Madeline/Judy—they all are structured by the void left by the absent Thing (God, the natural figure, the original wife).[20] It is this environment of lack that in the end seduces Scottie.

Opposed to this process of sublimation is the reversed movement where the outside hole is internalized by the subject himself. This internalization of lack defines the very process of mourning that dominates the second half of the film. After Madeline climbs a tower and apparently kills herself, thus showing how the ultimate extension of the death drive destroys the love object, Scottie goes through a period of mourning that borders on melancholia. In order to determine what psychological state Scottie is in, after Madeline's apparent death, we can turn to the essay "Mourning and Melancholia," where Freud distinguishes between the "normal" state of mourning a lost object and the "pathological" state of melancholia by insisting that in the latter, the subject identifies with the lost object itself.[21] "The loss suffered by the melancholic is that of an object; according to what he says the loss is one in himself" (168). Thus, the melancholic subject not only has to mourn the loss of the one that is now dead or lost, but he also has to mourn the loss of his own self. Hitchcock allows us to make this connection between Madeline's loss and Scottie's loss of his self when he has this male subject redream the lost female subject's own dream.

In Scottie's dream, we first see Madeline's flowers, which now become alive and start to dance around; then there is an image of Carlotta with Gavin and himself. We are next shown her jewels, and the empty nameless grave that is followed by the image of Scottie's"decapitated" head. Finally in the dream, we see Scottie falling down into an abyss in the same way that Madeline falls when she supposedly kills herself. This last image clearly depicts the way that Scottie has now identified with the lost object—he is no longer trying to hide his own nothingness by projecting it onto the female subject, but rather he is living this nothingness himself.

This male subject's identification with the lost object is emphasized by the fact that after Madeline commits suicide, he has lost his ability to speak and he remains silent and immobile in a hospital. By becoming the solitary object that sits and stares into nothingness, Scottie's presence has become reduced to being a pure gaze or stain that looks but doesn't see anything.[22] In fact, the dominant image of his dream is his own face that stares blankly into the camera. This image of the gaze connects to the beginning of the film, when we see a staring woman's eye and to the end of the film where Scottie tells Judy Barton that she was a very "apt Pupil."

A Very Apt Pupil

In the last part of the film, Scottie wants to bring Judy back to the scene of the crime in order to overcome his own loss and to become free of the past. Freedom is thus once again attached to the masculine desire to efface the Real by Symbolizing it and returning to a past event and reversing it in the structure of the death drive. Scottie now fully identifies with the part of Mr. Elster, who controls the signifier, and like him, he is going to force Judy up the tower to overcome his own fear of the abyss.

Scottie is not only repeating, but he also is returning and reversing. In *The Four Fundamental Concepts of Psychoanalysis*, Lacan argues that in the structure of the death drive, the subject attempts to reverse on a Symbolic level his or her own initial trauma and passivity (178, 183, 189, 206, 240). In this sense, instead of Scottie being the passive, anxious one, now it is Judy who becomes anxiety-stricken.

Scottie tells Judy that she did a good job, but she forgot one thing and that is Carlotta's necklace. He blames this lapse on her sentimentality, which prevents her from taking control of the drive itself. For one of the key functions of the death drive and the general structure of perversion is the overcoming not only of the subject's history, but also of sentimentality, especially the sentiments of shame, fear, and pity.[23] The jewel represents the insistence of the affect and the reminder of the Real Thing that has been effaced.

Doubling this insistence of the jewel is the presence of the female look or gaze that opens up the film. While climbing up the tower, Scottie repeats "You must have been a very apt pupil." Once again there is a double meaning to this line—she was a very good student in following Mr. Elster's directions, and she remained a very good eye, because she would not let her gaze be effaced.

Coupled with this highlighting of the female gaze at the end of the film, we find Scottie's realization that Judy's character was directed and controlled by Gavin Elster. As they climb up to the top of the tower, he exclaims to her: "Did he train you? Rehearse You? Did he tell you exactly what to do? What to say?" These lines can be directed towards both Hitchcock himself and Gavin. After all, it was Hitchcock who rehearsed and trained this female subject. The ending thus represents a profound self-awareness of the director's role in shaping and killing off the female subject.

Vertigo's self-reflexiveness displays Hitchcock's realization that the process of filmmaking partakes in the masculine usage of the Symbolic death drive. By revealing the inner-workings of this process, Hitchcock is able to turn the death drive back on itself and allow for what Lacan calls the true awareness of life itself:

> How can man, that is to say a living being, have access to knowledge of the death instinct, to his own relationship to death? The answer is by virtue of the signifier in its most radical form. It is in the signifier and insofar as the subject articulates a signifying chain that he comes up against the fact that he may disappear from the chain of what he is. (295)

Lacan's argument here affirms that the subject's awareness of the workings of the Symbolic death drive allow him to see that not only his object, but his self, is effaced by language. I am using the masculine pronoun here to stress the possibility that this theory of linguistic melancholia may pertain primarily to the male subject.

For if all acts of sublimation and linguistic representation are fueled by the male subject's attempt to separate from the realm of the maternal Thing and the gaping hole of the female genitalia, we may question if this same relationship to death is applicable to the female subject?[24] More so, if the male subject projects his own sense of nothingness onto the figure of the female subject, does this mean that women themselves identify with this position of nothingness and lack? In turning to *Marnie* in the next chapter, I will respond to these questions by examining the structures of sublimation and melancholia from the perspective of feminine subjectivity. From this angle, we can treat *Marnie* as a feminist reading of *Vertigo*.

6

Marnie: Abjection, Marking, and Feminine Subjectivity

Most of Hitchcock's films that I have been analyzing have centered on the exploration of masculine subjectivity and sexuality. In these films, bi-textuality has continuously been associated with the presence of the feminine form. With *Marnie*, we are able to explore the other side of bi-textuality and sexual representation. In this film, the displaced horror of feminine sexuality is displayed by a woman who experiences her own desire as a form of abjection. In this structure, Marnie is a woman who has internalized the dominant Symbolic order's rejection of feminine fluids and bi-textual desires.

As I have previously argued, the abjection and horror of feminine sexuality is most often related to a displacement and projection of bi-textual desire onto the debased realm of feminine sexuality. In this structure, men and women reject their own bisexuality because this undifferentiated form of Real desire threatens the very logic of the Symbolic binary order of sexual difference. In recent psychoanalytic and feminist theory, this displacement of the Real onto the feminine has resulted in the equation of the unconscious with a feminine form of writing and a definition of feminine subjectivity that is centered on the unknowability of the Real natural body.[1] More so, the recent theories of feminine writing (*écriture féminine*) that have been presented by Luce Irigaray, Julia Kristeva, and Hélène Cixous all participate in this transformation of the unconscious and the Real into the domain of the feminine.

Throughout her *Bodies that Matter*, Judith Butler returns to this question of feminizing the Real.[2] Butler has insisted that many theorists equate gender with the masculine attempt to construct sexual difference, while sex itself is relegated to the domain of a pre-discursive feminine Real:

> One question that feminists have raised, then, is whether the discourse that figures the action of construction as a kind of imprinting or imposition is not tacitly masculinist, whereas the figure of the passive surface, awaiting that penetrating act whereby meaning is endowed, is not tacitly or—perhaps—quite obviously feminine. Is sex to gender as feminine is to masculine?" (5)

Butler challenges this distinction between gender and sex in order to resist any attempt to equate feminine sexuality with the natural realm of the unsymbolizable Real:

> Indeed as much as the radical distinction between sex and gender has been crucial to the de Beauvoirian version of feminism, it has come under criticism in more recent years for degrading the natural as that which is "before" intelligibility, in need of the mark, if not the mar, of the social to signify, to be known, to acquire value (4–5).

In the case of *Marnie*, we find that the female subject is marked and marred by the Symbolic order that attempts to render her visible.

Like the other films that I have investigated, Hitchcock's exploration of the relationship between the marring and marking of the feminine subject is produced on the level of a bi-textual unconscious discourse. Throughout his films, we re-find in the names of his female characters the insistence of the letters "MAR."[3] In *Jamaica Inn*, there is Mary, in *Dial M for Murder*, Margot, in *Spellbound*, Mary, in *Psycho*, Marion and Mary, and in *Marnie*, Margaret, Marion, Martha, Mary, and Marnie. The Mar symbol condenses together the two words Mark and Mar, and points to the ways that the mark of language serves to replace or Symbolically murder the original Thing for the subject.[4] Furthermore, this unconscious insistence on the marring effects of language in Hitchcock's work is most often attached to feminine characters and the presence of feminine sexuality. Thus, Hitchcock's films participate in the cultural process of gendering the relationship between language and the Real.

Throughout *Marnie*, the character of Mark Rutland (Sean Connery) will be associated with the marking effects of language, while Marnie (Tippi Hedren) will be connected to the ways that the feminine subject is marred by masculine sexuality and discourse. This gendered distinction between the Symbolic mark and the marring of the Real can be read as a normative description of the dominant cultural order. However, I would like to examine the ways that Hitchcock's own film both supports and challenges this strict binary logic.

Self-Abjection

Marnie represents a female subject who has a horror of her own sexuality. From a certain perspective, we can argue that this woman has internalized her culture's own abjection and rejection of feminine sexuality and subjectivity. In order to explore this process of self-abjection, I will turn towards Julia Kristeva's theory of the "abject" in her *Powers of Horror: An Essay on Abjection*.[5] Kristeva begins her discussion of this psychological state by describing a general experience of abjection:

> There looms, within abjection, one of those violent, dark revolts of being, directed against a threat that seems to emanate from an exorbitant outside or inside, ejected beyond the scope of the possible, the tolerable, and the thinkable. (1)

In Marnie's case, this production of the unthinkable threat of abjection is tied to the presence of red spots on a white surface. Like John Ballantine from *Spellbound*, who cannot tolerate the sight of black lines on a white surface, Marnie's anxiety is also linked to the scene of writing and feminine sexuality. At one moment in the film, Marnie spills red ink on her white blouse and she begins to panic. We can interpret this red ink that horrifies her as a symbol of her own feminine fluids. In this way, Marnie represents an internalization of the horror of the feminine that we have witnessed in so many of Hitchcock's other films.

Linked to Marnie's anxiety over the red writing substance on a white surface is her general rejection of men and her attempt to remain virginal. In the film, she will marry Mark Rutland but refuse to have sex with him. This refusal of playing by the rules of the dominant heterosexual order is also tied in the film to her own sense of self-revulsion. In this structure, this feminine subject not only rejects the desire of the masculine Other but, more importantly, she also rejects her own desire and sexuality. Since the production of masculine desire is tied to the equation of femininity with natural fluids, Marnie's rejection of her own fluids implies a rejection of the Symbolic order of identification. In Kristeva's reading of this dynamic, she posits that the (female) subject who rejects the dominant forms of identification is left with no choice but to identify with the abject object itself:

> When that subject, weary of fruitless attempts to identify with something on the outside, finds the impossible within: when it finds that the impossible constitutes its very being, that it is none other than abject. The abjection of self would be the culminating form of that experience to which is revealed that all its objects are based merely on the inaugural loss that laid the foundation of its being. (5)

In this structure of self-abjection, the subject identifies directly with the objects that are excluded by the imposition of the Symbolic order onto the Real. My hypothesis is that when Marnie panics in front of the red marks on a white surface, she is reacting to her own identification with these excluded Real fluids.

While Kristeva does not equate the abject here to the presence of the feminine, it is clear that the female resistance to the master signifier often places women in the position of being themselves the abject object. "From its place of banishment, the abject does not cease challenging its master.

Without a sign (for him) it beseeches a discharge, a convulsion, a crying out" (2). In Lacan's theory of the discourse of the hysteric, this constant challenge by the object to the master is indicated by the opposition between the object (*a*) and the master signifier (S1):

$$\frac{\$}{a} \xrightarrow{\hspace{1cm}} \frac{S1}{S2}$$

This structure shows in part how the hysteric's symptoms (S1), complaints, and protests to the Other are caused by the encounter with the object (*a*) that serves to split the subject (\$) and force her or him to find a signifier (S1) in the Other.[6] We shall see how this process is at the very heart of the film *Marnie*.

Throughout the film, Marnie continuously resists the desire of all of the men around her. Her refusal of her own sexuality, in turn, undermines the desire of the Other, which only pushes them to desire her even more. This feminine resistance to the desire of the masculine Other ties into Kristeva's notion of the way that the subject of abjection serves to disturb all forms of "identity, system and order" (4). Due to the fact that this subject is linked to an object that is excluded by the Symbolic order, any attempt of the subject to identify with the abject causes a threat to the different social power structures. Kristeva insists that this subject, "does not respect borders, positions, rules. [She is] The in-between, the ambiguous, the composite. The traitor, the liar, the criminal with a good conscience" (4). This passage perfectly describes Marnie who is shown to move from one place to the other, to change jobs, to take on new identities and to steal and lie, while at the same time she takes on a hyper-moral attitude towards her own sexuality.

Kristeva's theory of the abject subject allows us to reconcile many of the contradictions that run through this film and its commentary.[7] One problem that past critics have dealt with is precisely Marnie's combination of sexual hyper-morality (frigidity) and criminal activity. Is she a sexual hysteric or is she a perverse kleptomaniac? We don't have to choose between these two options because she is both in one—she steals in order to challenge the law that has determined her sexuality and presence to be outside of the Symbolic order.

From this perspective, when she steals money from men, what she is really stealing is their control of the master signifier. In this sense, she does not have penis-envy, but rather she has phallus-envy. She wants to take the power-signifier from the Other in order to prevent men from controlling her as an object. This link between stealing and her resistance to men becomes evident after she gives her mother a fur and she states, "Oh, we don't need men, mama. We can do very well for ourselves, just you and me." We shall see that Marnie's plea to her mother is based on a desire to resist the desire of the men that surround her.

The rejection of the Other, in the process of identifying with the abject object, allows the feminine subject a profound awareness of the way that language serves to negate and kill off the original Thing or object. Kristeva argues that the peak of the experience of the abject is when the subject realizes that her own being is defined by this state of nothingness. In Marnie's case, what her abjection proves is the very lack that is at the center of the dominant order. By holding onto the object and the bodily flow that is originally excluded by language and society, this female subject is able to dig a hole in the place of the Other.

Feminine Presence and the Hole in the Other

This presence of the hole and the female object becomes evident in the very beginning of the film. In the first scene, we see Marnie holding a purse that has a vaginal shape, then in the next scene we see an empty safe, and we hear a masculine voice exclaim the word "robbed!" This movement articulates the transition from the presence of the abject object (a) in the form of the vaginal purse, to the lacking subject (S— the empty safe), to the signifier of loss (S1—robbed!) in the place of the Other. On the level of the discourse of the hysteric, Marnie is the abject-object that refuses all signifiers and thus causes the Other to mark her absence with a symptomatic exclamation of loss. She literally "robs" the male subjects of the foundations to their sexuality and subjectivity by stealing their money and their ability to name things.

This dialectical progression from presence, to absence and finally to the naming of the presence of absence runs throughout the film. In the scene that follows the discovery of her robbery, we see Marnie return to a hotel room, where she changes her hair color and begins to pack. We watch as she takes out a make-up compact and removes the mirror from it, in order to get to the stack of fake social security cards that she has placed behind it. All of the names on these cards (Marion, Mary, Margaret, Martha) begin with the letters "M-a-r," and I would argue that they all point to the letteral insistence of her identity. Her abjection is represented by the way that this mark of being marred returns in each of the names that she takes from the Other. Furthermore, Hitchcock shows himself to be a good Lacanian by placing the Symbolic names of the Other beyond and behind the mirror of Imaginary relations.[8]

In the dialectical structure of this losing and taking on the name of the Other, Marnie highlights the way that identity can be constructed through the Symbolic name. Due to the fact that her own self is experienced as a pure nothingness or lack, she is able to fill that lack by stealing Other signifiers.[9] During one point in the film, we are told that she has "no references." This could mean not only that she has no past, but also that she does not refer to anything in particular. She is able to reconstruct herself on the level of the signifier, precisely because she has divorced language from any extra-referential capability.[10]

Of course, thematically, Marnie takes on other names because she is trying to escape the past, but her very name points to the insistence of the impossibility to completely repress her early trauma. She is marred and marked by her mother and her repressed awareness that she has killed a man and that her mother was a prostitute. What then will not let her forget or what causes her anxiety is the return of the letters "mar" and the red spots on white surfaces.

In the scene where Marnie drops red ink on herself and then desperately attempts to wash it away, this stain serves to link together writing, blood, and memory. In order to efface the past she has to efface the very possibility of representation itself. The red is the color that not only marks her initial crime, but also points to a loss of virginity. It is the stain of the impure and the unnamed. However, in Hitchcock's world nothing can be completely effaced; every crime and desire leaves behind an indelible mark or letter.

This insistence of a form of writing and marking that refuses to be effaced is brought out in the film by the bank worker who can never remember the code to the safe, so he must constantly refer to a book where the code is written down. In other words, even if the subject of the unconscious forgets or denies a word or event, it is always written down somewhere else, in the place of the Other.[11] Writing is therefore a key to the ethical unconscious because it retains the residues of the truth that the subject attempts to repress.

Marking and Tracking

Opposed to this emergence of the feminine mark of writing, we find in the film the character Mark Rutland, who is constantly reading about women and the animal kingdom. Rutland desires to tame and control Marnie as if she were some animal that needed to be domesticated. Mark tells her that he is interested in zoology and female instincts and in this way, she comes to represent some natural force that men need to contain or it will control them. Rutland exhorts at one point "I tracked you and I caught you and by God I'm going to keep you." This notion of tracking here can refer not only to the way that he hunts her down, but also to the process of "tracking" in film. Hitchcock, the director, has tracked and trapped Marnie, the female object. By being represented in film, her own essence is denied and she becomes effaced by the structure of the signifier. Furthermore, this play on the word "tracking" serves to identify Rutland with Hitchcock, and thus the exploration of Rutland's attempt to understand and contain Marnie can be equated with the director's attempt to contain and control the feminine form.

However, as I have previously pointed out, Hitchcock's position in his own films is often ambiguous and multidimensional. In fact, I would like to insist that his identifications are most often structured by a fundamental form of bi-sexuality.[12] In this film, we can not simply equate the director with the leading male protagonist, but we must also seek out his identification with the female lead. Therefore, in the same way that Freud posits a universal foundation of bisexuality in every subject's unconscious, we can seek out the bisexuality of film representation and the way that this sexuality and textuality is repressed and transformed.

In her introduction to *The Women Who Knew Too Much*, Tania Modleski argues that, "in Hitchcock's films, the strong fascination and identification with femininity revealed in them subverts the claims to mastery and authority not only of the male characters but of the director himself" (3). I would add to this that Hitchcock's "over-identification" with his female characters is most explicit in a film like *Marnie*, where so much of the narrative is dependent on a female subject's presence and actions.

In fact, in the early scene where we watch Marnie change her hair color and take on a new name, we also find several references to Hitchcock's own presence. While Marnie is walking back to her room, we see the director himself walk out of a door and stare briefly into the camera. This use of the director's look that gazes at the audience serves to reverse for an instant the normal situation where the director's gaze is hidden behind the camera. Instead of the audience being equated with the point of view of this male director, Hitchcock splits the relation between vision and the gaze, and allows himself to be the gaze-object of the audience's point of view.[13] By placing his gaze in front of the camera, Hitchcock refuses to let his real presence be effaced through the process of representation. In this way, he becomes a reminder of the lost Thing and a representative of the unconscious.

Another indication of this connection between Marnie's identity and Hitchcock's presence can be found when Marnie enters her hotel room and starts to pack her suitcases. In one of her cases, we find a large box with the name "Albert's" on it. This name is a recurrent theme in Hitchcock's films and I believe that it is a play on the director's own name "Alfred."[14] While Marnie does not choose to take on this name herself, she does contain it in the suitcase with which she travels. In other words, among her own set of signifiers and symbols, she has Hitchcock's own displaced identity. Likewise, by placing himself in the scene of Marnie's own self-construction, Hitchcock attaches his identity to the dispersement of Symbolic identifications. As Modleski insists, this dispersement or multiplication of possible names and identities serves, in turn, to decenter the director's narrative control. His own text becomes polymorphously diverse as it alludes to a wide-range of different forms of sexuality, as well as, textuality.

We do not know in the film if Marnie is a heterosexual woman who hates men, or if is she a lesbian that prefers women, or if she identifies with being a man who loves women, or a bisexual who desires everyone or no one. The multiplicity of her possible sexual desires is matched by the endless varieties of Hitchcock's own subjective positions. However, if as Modleski suggests, we can "implicitly challenge and decenter directorial authority by considering Hitchcock's work as the expression of cultural attitudes and practices existing to some extent outside the artist's control" (3), we must still account for the way that his work is recentered and the way that diverse forms of textuality and sexuality are contained and reappropriated.

In other terms, if Hitchcock does indeed produce a body of work that opens up a diverse realm of sexuality and textuality, why have his films most often been received as moralistic glorifications of a centered-heterosexual-white-male-author? The answer to this question would seem to lie in the reception of his work and the way that we read texts and films in general. Theories of spectatorship would appear to be the privileged place for a discussion of the production of monological readings of these multi-logical texts. Yet, it becomes clear through Modleski's discussion of the history of film theory that theories of spectatorship have often been a source for the narrowing of the field of reception.

Where a promise for greater diversity in interpretation does seem to be alive is in the recent theories of bisexual identification. Modleski mentions Teresa de Lauretis's conception of "double desire" as a mode of spectatorship that allows for a desire that is "both passive and active, homosexual and heterosexual" (6). Furthermore, Modleski turns to Anne Kaplan's discussion of Kristeva's semiotic theory to argue that "patriarchy must repress the nonsymbolic aspects of motherhood because of the 'homosexual components' involved in the mother/daughter relationship" (7). This last theory helps to explain why diverse aspects of Hitchcock's works are most often repressed; the dominant social order cannot tolerate the threat of bisexual desire and multitextuality. In order to contain these threatening forces, the male subject and the larger social structure must read these texts and subjectivities on the level of a monological "compulsory heterosexuality." Reading and viewing are thus major forces that allow for the stabilization of the dominant ideologies and political systems. To attempt to read in a way that highlights the diversity of texts and sexualities is, in this sense, a political act in itself.[15]

Identification, Abjection, and the Real

Before we get to an explicit discussion of the bisexual nature of *Marnie*, I would like to return to Kristeva's notion of abjection to help to account for the way that multiple forms of textuality and sexuality become excluded and silenced. This theory will allow us to articulate the way that masculinity and femininity are constructed out of an initial state of subjective indeterminacy. Of course, identification is the classical psychoanalytic concept that helps to explain the way that different forms of subjectivity are constituted. However, we learn from Kristeva that the flip side of identification is abjection, just as the dialectical opposite of the signifier is the abject-object.

Due to the fact that Marnie's mother has prayed for her to be given the "gift of forgetting" and has constantly refused to be affectionate towards her, Marnie is placed in the position of the abject-subject who "has swallowed up instead of maternal love . . . a maternal hatred without a word for the words of the father" (6). The only thing that Marnie has identified with is her mother's hatred of men and her desire to no longer be circulated in the masculine-controlled economy of desire and money. Her identification is thus not on the level of an Imaginary maternal relation, nor on the level of a Symbolic form of law and discourse, but rather on the basis of an excluded Real object.

In an essay entitled "Identification and the Real," Kristeva outlines a theory of primary identification, which I believe can help us to establish a non-Symbolic and non-Imaginary form of subjective construction and identification.[16] "Far from being a simple equivalent to the signifier of the Symbolic schema, it involves the Real, and particularly the body. The symptom may be an identification made flesh, through refusing to submit to the demand for identity dictated by frustrations and language" (167). This primary form of Real identification, which can be located on the level of the material body, represents a resistance to the structured world of identity and language. In Marnie's case, this lack of identity is presented by the way that she takes on several different names, changes her hair color several times, and lies about her past.

Marnie's multiplicity of identities points to what Kristeva calls "crossed identifications," which imply in themselves a bisexual form of identifying and becoming one with the Other. By cross-identifying, the female subject "identifies with both her father and her mother, pleasure and disappearance, rigidity and absence, phallic power and death" (169). Marnie is powerful in the way that she takes on the major signifiers of the male world—she renames herself and steals money from men. Yet, she is also powerless because she cannot stay in one place or stick to one identity. This combination of masculine control and feminine movement can be traced back to the primal scene and her Oedipus Complex.

In the flashback scene where we watch Marnie kill a sailor who has tried to seduce her and is fighting with her mother, we see a classic reenactment of the (negative) Oedipus Complex. The daughter hates the father for sleeping with her mother, so she attempts to get rid of him. However, instead of this feminine subject simply repressing the existence of her father by identifying with the desire of her mother, she literally kills off the Symbolic father figure. She therefore takes a figurative structure and translates it into a literal event. In other words, she attempts to constitute her subjectivity through a Real act, not a Symbolic representation.

This constant attempt by this female subject to resist Symbolic structures in an effort to reestablish a relationship to the Real, helps to explain one of the problems in Freud's conception of feminine sexuality. In his theory of feminine development, Freud argues that the female subject must learn to exchange her "masculine" clitoral enjoyment for the passive "feminine" pleasures of the vagina as well as give up her real attachment to the mother and take on a Symbolic connection to her father.[17] The giving up of the clitoris and the giving up of the mother are therefore both linked together for the female subject. These Real, material forms of enjoyment and bodily contact are set in opposition to the more distant and abstract Symbolic figures of the father and the vagina. One could argue that for Freud, the vagina can be considered to be a Symbolic structure because it is thoroughly contained within the social discourse of puberty and the desire of the Other.[18]

Furthermore, in Freud's developmental model, the female subject has to be forced to give up the excitement that she gains from the stimulation of her clitoris, in order to find excitement in the realm of the Other.[19] The double threat of feminine sexuality for a masculine-dominated society is that (1) the female subject will gain too much satisfaction from stimulating her own sexual organ; and (2) she will prefer to stay with the sex of her original love-object, the mother. To overcome the clitoris and to overcome the mother, thus, also means to overcome lesbian desire. Furthermore, all of these acts of overcoming are all based on the feminine acceptance of castration that implies the overvaluation of the male figure (the phallus) and the degradation of the female form (the vagina).

While we cannot assert with any certainty that Hitchcock wants to place Marnie in the position of being a lesbian, we do know that she cannot stand to have men handle her in any way. In fact, it seems that the only one that she has any sexual feelings towards is her horse, who she admonishes in the film by stating that, "If you want to bite someone, bite me." It may be trite to bring up here the autoerotic pleasures that the female subject receives from horseback riding, however it is clear that Marnie enjoys having a horse between her legs, more than a man. Rutland indicates this when he says to his father, "She's not a girl, just a horse-fancier."

To counter or appropriate Marnie's love of horses, Mark tries to use her animal lust in order to get her to fall in love with him. First he does this by taking her to a horse race, but this attempt fails once she sees a jockey who has red spots on his shirt. In another effort to seduce her, he kisses her in a barn. Here we have the transference effect that Freud attaches to the movement between the clitoris and the vagina. "When at least the sexual act is permitted and the clitoris itself becomes excited, it still retains a function: the task, namely, of transmitting the excitation to the adjacent female sexual parts, just as—to use a simile—pine shavings can be kindled in order to set a log of harder wood on fire" (87). In Freud's theory, clitoral excitement can only be justified if it serves to excite the vagina and thus prepare the female subject for her male partner. Likewise, Rutland tries to excite Marnie by bringing her near horses and then hoping that her excitement will spread to him.

In another scene, Mark has Marnie go on a fox hunt with her father, but once again she becomes repulsed when she sees a dead fox and the red jackets that the other (male) riders are wearing. The transference of her excitement is here blocked by the association between men and blood. For she unconsciously remembers seeing the red blood on the murdered sailor's white uniform. In a final attempt to gain Marnie's love, Rutland buys her a horse. She then goes off to ride, but the horse stumbles while jumping over a fence. Due to the extent of the injury, she is left with no choice, but to shoot the horse herself. After she puts the horse out of its misery, she says "There, now" which is exactly the same thing that she says after she kills the sailor. The primal scene is thus repeated and transformed by the horse taking on the role of the sailor—by killing the animal, instead of the man, she is able to overcome her need to steal and to refuse Rutland.

The killing of the horse represents the killing off of her own sexual enjoyment. In order for her to be integrated into Mark Rutland's masculine order, she has to give up the pleasure that she receives from this animal. In the scene following the horse shooting, she attempts to rob Rutland again, but this time her hand cannot reach out and touch the money.

In the scenes of the murdering of the horse and of the sailor, it is essential that Marnie has to carry out the act herself. By being the agent of death and by killing her own love-object, Marnie shows that she has internalized the death drive of the Other. For Kristeva, the very process of abjection is tied to this internalization of the Symbolic Other: "A heterogeneous flux marks out a territory that I can call my own because the Other, having dealt in me as alter ego, points it out to me through loathing" (10). I believe that Kristeva is arguing here that the only way that one can experience one's own difference and heterogeneity is by a form of self-loathing that comes from the internalized social Other.

Marnie brings out this element of self-abjection when she refuses Rutland's sexual advances by stating, "I'm not like other people, I know what I am." She can only locate her true being outside of the Other, yet she has a horror of her own self. In the paradoxical nature of the abject-subject, self-awareness is tied to self-hatred. This internalization of self-abjection can be considered to be one of the major ways that the social system is able to control the subject's diverse sexuality and textuality.[20]

At the end of the film, Marnie declares to Rutland, "I don't want to go to jail, I'd rather stay with you." Her absorption into the male-controlled heterosexual order has thus been completed, but this process can only be realized through the threat of punishment and containment. Her choice is what Lacan would call a "forced-choice," and it reflects on the way that we are socialized to read texts and our selves on the level of deadly choices between identification and abjection.

Kristeva's theory of abjection has helped us to interpret one of the main ways that the dominant Symbolic order is able to repress multiple aspects of bi-textuality. By internalizing the hatred that language has for the non-Symbolized Real body, Marnie becomes a victim to the heterosexist demand for sexual submission. However, in her early attempts to identify with this Real aspect of sexuality and identity, she is able to place her being on the outskirts of the phallo-centric masculine realm. Thus, Hitchcock produces and contains a radical form of feminine resistance. This ambivalent structure points to his own cross-identifications and directorial bi-textuality.

7

Rear Window Ethics: Laura Mulvey
and the Inverted Gaze

The film *Rear Window* has been used as the paradigmatic example of the masculine control over the visual field.
This argument was perhaps first made by Laura Mulvey in
her article "Visual Pleasure and Narrative Cinema."[1] While
this essay contains one of the most influential arguments in
feminist film theory, I will argue that Mulvey not only
reverses Lacan's notions of the gaze and voyeurism, but that
she also fails to see one of Hitchcock's most radical investiga-
tions of bi-textuality and the ethics of representation. Her
own misreading, then, becomes a starting place for a continuous series of misreadings and misappropriations of Lacan's
work by other feminist scholars.

The Turning Around of the Gaze

Often in feminist film theory, the "gaze" is considered to
be equivalent to the (masculine) control of the visual field.
On its most basic level, these theories argue that men control women by making them the object of their visual intent.
Likewise, voyeurism is treated as the sexual equivalent of
this masculine control of vision. However, a careful reading
of Lacan's definitions of both the gaze and voyeurism shows
that he means something very different by these notions. In
fact, his usage of these concepts is in virtual opposition to

their common feminist treatment. By correcting this reversal of the usage of the gaze and voyeurism, I will not be trying to undermine diverse feminist arguments; rather, I will try to strengthen them by giving them a more radical and fundamental foundation.

In *Lacan's Four Fundamental Concepts of Psychoanalysis*, it is clear that he most often refers to the gaze in a situation where vision is either limited or blocked.[2] In one of his earliest arguments, he sets up a binary opposition between the intentionality of an individual's control of vision and his own notion of the look or gaze.[3] "I see only from one point, but in my existence I am looked at from all sides" (72). Here the opposition is similar to the relation that Sartre describes in *Being and Nothingness*.[4] As an ego of consciousness, I decide what I want to look at and what I want to see (I have only one point of view), but as an object of the look or gaze of the Other, I am looked at from all angles.

In Sartre's discussion of this structure, he describes a situation where he enters a park and sees the trees that he always sees and the bench that he always sees—all is ordered and structured by his intentionality and the direction of his vision. However, if suddenly a man appears and looks back at Sartre, he is no longer in control and he is now the object of the other's look. We can call this a "reversal of consciousness," just as Freud describes the unconscious as the reverse of the conscious system.[5]

In other terms, when Lacan states that I see from one point, but I am looked at from all sides, he is indicating that there is an inverse relation between the one who is looking and the one who is looked at. Furthermore, he places the subject that is looked at in the position of the object (*a*) in the form of the gaze.

For Lacan, the gaze itself is an example of the "lack that constitutes castration anxiety" (73). This indicates that the inverse relation between vision and the gaze is doubled by the binary opposition between the phallus and castration. In Lacan's theory, the gaze proves castration by undermining the visual presence of the phallus and the mastery of the visual field. "In our relation to things, in so far as this relation is constituted by the way of vision, and ordered in the

[handwritten margin notes: "gaze is limited"; "looking back = reversal of conscious of control"]

figures of representation, something slips, passes, is trans-
mitted, from stage to stage, and is always to some degree
eluded in it—that is what we call the gaze" (73). The gaze is
therefore the object that is eluded by all forms of representation and vision; it is the lack or the limit that is inscribed
into the phenomenology of consciousness.

If we now look at Mulvey's article, we find out that the
presence of the gaze has also eluded her representation.
Such phrases as "the determining male gaze projects its
phantasy onto the female figure" (33), or "she holds the look,
plays to and signifies male desire" (33), show a confusion
between the gaze and the eye of vision that Lacan attempts
to split apart.

[margin note: gaze vs. eye of vision.]

In Mulvey's theory, men need to present women in a
castrated form by controlling and dictating their image.
Moreover, in film, Mulvey insists that male viewers identify
with the male protagonist, who controls the movement of the
female image and body. "As the spectator identifies with the
main male protagonist, he projects his look onto that of his
like, his screen surrogate, so that the power of the male protagonist as he controls events coincides with the active
power of the erotic look, both giving a satisfying sense of
omnipotence (34)." Once again, in this structure, the look is
something that a male figure can control and project, and
not as Lacan articulates it, an object that threatens to escape
from the control of the eye or the 'I.'

In her article, Mulvey applies this inverted usage of the
gaze to an analysis of *Rear Window*. She argues that
"Hitchcock's skillful use of identification processes and lib-
eral use of subjective camera from the point of view of the
male protagonist draw the spectators deeply into his position, making them share his uneasy gaze" (37). The gaze of
the viewer is therefore made to be equivalent to the male
protagonist's gaze and ultimately to Hitchcock's own gaze
that controls the camera. Our feeling of power, then, comes
from Hitchcock's own ability to control the action and the
forms that are presented on the screen. I will soon show how
if this is the case, Hitchcock radically fails at his control of
the visual world.

What Does the Voyeur See?

Another problem with Mulvey's use of psychoanalytic theory is her use of the term "voyeurism." Mulvey insists that in *Vertigo*, the Jimmy Stewart character is a voyeur, because "he falls in love with a woman he follows and spies on without speaking to (37). For Mulvey, the voyeur can only maintain his drive if he looks at his object of beauty without speaking to it. This inability to interact with the sexual object, however, seems more indicative of a neurotic inhibition than a perverse form of voyeurism.

Clearly, Mulvey unlike Freud and Lacan, places, voyeurism in the field of neurosis and not perversion. "Thus the two looks materially present in time and space are obsessively subordinated to the neurotic needs of the male ego" (39). What Mulvey is in reality describing here is the structure of narcissism and not that of voyeurism. The narcissistic subject needs to reinforce its ego by finding ideal images and forms that reinforce its own sense of ideal formation and bodily coherency. One could then argue that what Hitchcock attempts to project onto the screen are ideal objects of beauty, which satisfy our own narcissistic demands for ideal forms.

However, for Lacan, the gaze as a form of the object (a) is always without a specular image and thus represents an inversion of narcissism. This object does not give one a sense of visual totality or control and therefore a sense of bodily integration; rather, the gaze-object serves to fragment the illusion of the totalized body-image. Likewise, for Lacan, voyeurism is predicated on the presentation of the unseen object that undermines the intentionality of the ego:

> What he is trying to see, make no mistake, is the object as absence. What the voyeur is looking for and finds is merely a shadow behind the curtain. . . . What he is looking for is not, as one says, the phallus—but precisely its absence (182).

In other words, what the voyeur is looking to see is the absence of the ideal image or phallus and not its presence.

[handwritten margin notes: "narcissism not voyeurism" and "Looking for absence, for phallus the actual object not"]

The male voyeur thus looks into the place of the Other, not to see the ideal image of the woman, but rather to see her absence.

If we now read Lacan's theory back into Mulvey's analysis, we find that the important aspect of the structure of film vision is not the way that the director or male protagonist holds the female object under their intended point of view, but rather the way that the feminine object looks at the male subject from a position of unrepresentibility. In this structure, the male figure attempts to dominate the female object, not by making her more visual, but rather by pushing her to the limits of the visible and the sayable.

We can begin our search for the gaze in *Rear Window* by analyzing the opening scene, which curiously shows the Jimmy Stewart character, L. B. Jefferies, looking away from an open window, asleep, as the camera pans various photographs on his wall that depict images of destruction. This is hardly a man who is actively pursuing images through his window; in fact, he is not active at all, because he has been rendered immobile by a body cast. In a way, L. B. Jefferies is the inactive and passive object that is stuck in Hitchcock's cast. More so, on his cast we see the following words written, "Here lies the broken bones of L. B. Jefferies." Before the film even begins, the actor is already dead.

The negativity of this opening scene is further enhanced by a strange picture of his beloved, Lisa, the Grace Kelly character. What is interesting about this image is that it is not a developed photograph, but rather a reversed negative. We can read this object as a fore-shadowing of Lisa's own negative presence before she is exposed and transformed into an image of perfection. Lisa's connection to negativity and inversion is brought out in her first appearance, when she approaches L. B. J. As she moves towards him, the camera shows her dark shadow moving across his face. Once again in this structure, Jefferies is in a passive position and Lisa is presented as being an active figure that approaches the male figure through the presentation of a negative object (the shadow).[6]

We must remember that in Lacan's theory of voyeurism, what the voyeur looks to see is the shadow of the Other because shadows make present a certain absence (182). Furthermore, Lacan indicates that if the Other is reduced to being a shadow, the subject can fantasize "any magic of presence" that he or she so desires:

> What the voyeur is looking for and finds is merely a shadow, a shadow behind a curtain. There he will fantasize any magic of presence, the most graceful of girls, for example, even if on the other side there is only a hairy athlete. . . . What one looks at is what cannot be seen. (182)

In Hitchcock's film, we actually do see "the most graceful of girls," Grace Kelly, so we may ask what is Jefferies really looking for? Could it be a hairy athlete?

Hind-Sight and Homo-Erotism

After all, one of the major subtexts of the film's dialogue is the question of why Jefferies does not want to marry Lisa. In part, we are led to believe that he is afraid of losing his mobility, even though in his present state, he is already immobile. Jefferies insists that he does not think that Lisa Freemont is the type of woman that can handle his line of work. However, can we not posit beneath this fear of immobility, a general fear of his own homosexual desires? Isn't the rear view that he is trying to see, precisely a view of another male figure that he suspects has killed his wife?

In his book *Looking Awry*, Slavoj Zizek has astutely pointed out that perhaps Jefferies' interest in the wife-killer's movements represents his own desire to kill off his own potential wife.[7] In Zizek's theory, it is the other (the killer) that realizes the desire of the subject (Jefferies). However, the motive for this desire is still left unexplained.

Perhaps we can partially account for Jefferies desire by looking at Lee Edelman's article, "Seeing Things: Representation, the Scene of Surveillance, and the Spectacle of Gay Male Sex."[8] Edelman argues that psychoanalytic theory is dominated by a certain level of "(be)hind-sight." Not only do analysts sit behind their patients, but they also attempt to determine why a certain event has a certain meaning by looking at the event retroactively or with hindsight. Furthermore, in Freud's Wolf Man case, the traumatic primal scene is posited as a view of his father entering his mother from behind. Edelman argues that Freud and his patient resist the acknowledgement of this anal erotic scene:

> The mere envisioning of this scene, with its spectacular representation of penetration from behind, may color or call into question the position of the analyst or even psychoanalysis itself—in relation to the man on the analyst's couch. (100)

From Edelman's angle, not only does Freud resist the homoerotic implications of being behind his male patients, but he also attempts to repress his own theory, which states that children believe that "sexual intercourse takes place at the anus" (101).

I would like to argue that the repression of this homoerotic primal scene and theory must affect all male subjects' later heterosexual object-choices. This could mean that the voyeur has to see the missing phallus in order to allow for a compromise formation between his or her heterosexual and homoerotic desires. By seeing the Other in the shadows and behind the curtain, the male viewer can imagine that the female subject does have the phallus, but not because he is afraid of losing his own, but because he secretly wants both a man and a woman. In *Rear Window*, we can thus rethink the relationship between Jefferies, Lisa, and the spectacle outside of his window, as a complicated circulation of both homosexual and heterosexual desires. What Jefferies wants to see is a certain absence that will block the presence of his own homosexual desire. This reading gains credence if we first look at the end of the film.

When Jefferies finally encounters the suspected killer, Lars Thorwald, he attempts to fight him off by flashing a camera light at him. His panic in front of this male figure results in his attempt to use his camera, not as a mode of reproducing an image, but rather as a way of blocking off representation. This blocking of representation would be indicative of the type of homosexual panic that Eve Kosofsky Sedgwick outlines in her book *Between Men: English Literature and Homosocial Desire.*[9] The confusion and disorder that may occur in a subject who begins to experience his own homosexual desires can be reflected in the upsetting of the visual field that *Rear Window* depicts. In order to prevent the surfacing of his true desire, Jefferies and by implication Hitchcock and the identifying audience, has to destroy the object of his view and immobilizes the object (a) or gaze.

If we return now to our previous discussion of the gaze and its opposition to the subject's point of view, we can begin to see why a subject may attempt to seek out an object that is placed at the limits of representation. The inverted relation between the gaze and the subjective view becomes an explicit theme in the film, when Jefferies' nurse exclaims that people ought to go out of their own houses and look inside. In other words, to reparaphrase Lacan, instead of people looking out and judging others from their single point of view, they should try to look at themselves from the position of the Other. An ethical way of looking would therefore represent an inversion of the intentional cogito, which thinks before it is and sees before it is looked at.

Jefferies not only has a horror of encountering his true desire, but he also is afraid of being looked at by the Other. These two fears would seem to go together if we figure that the omniscient Other knows what Jefferies really desires. His constant attempts then to avoid having the killer see him, also, represent his attempts at avoiding the acknowledgement of his repressed homosexuality.

Jefferies' desire to see the unseeable is not limited to his attempts at seeing what is going on in the suspected killers apartment. He is also interested in watching the female character that he names "Miss Lonely Heart." In one scene, we watch as this character prepares and consumes a romantic dinner with an absent partner. As we see her eating alone, but pretending that there is someone else with her, we hear in the background the singing of the words "To see you is to love you." While this popular song intones that love is based on the vision of the love object, the scene itself mocks this song by showing the object of love to be visually absent.

If we then affirm that this scene is a projection of Jefferies' desire, we once again are faced with a situation where he desires to see and to love the unrepresentable.

Another facet of Jefferies' identifications and projections is the way that his situation with Lisa parallels the initial relation between the killer and his wife. As Modleski and Hitchcock himself have pointed out, Jefferies in his cast is like the invalid wife, who we only see in her bed, while the free and mobile Lisa is like the killer who goes in and out of the apartment.[10] While Modleski stresses that this means that the female character is active and not passive as Mulvey insists, what she doesn't take into account is the possibility that Jefferies may want to be identified with the killer's wife in order to have an imagined relationship with a man. Furthermore, if Lisa is identified with the killer, her attempts at seducing Jefferies into marrying her must be considered from his point of view to be very much like an attempt of murder. This connection between murder and marriage in Hitchcock's work is constant, but here it takes on an extra force because it is attached to the subject's desire to deny his own bi-sexuality.

In light of this denial of homoerotism, we can wonder if Hitchcock's own compulsive heterosexual endings point to his repression of deeper sexual ambivalence. After all, the windows that we look through in this film seem to offer us an endless possibility of sexual relations and positions. In one apartment we have Miss Torso, the dancer, who is always surrounded by a group of men, but never seems to be happy. Likewise in another apartment we have a newly married couple, where the wife keeps on calling the husband back to bed. And in the killer's apartment, we first see his wife nagging at him, while he waves his hand at her. Perhaps all of these couples represent Jefferies' own projection of his fears about getting married.

In a central scene, the identification between Jefferies and the people on the other side of the courtyard becomes explicit. While Lisa is preparing his dinner, Jefferies is sitting at his window and looking out at different people's apartments. First he sees the killer's wife, who is also being served her dinner in bed. Then he next looks at Miss Lonely

Hearts, who is about to eat a meal alone. When she sits down and lifts her glass of wine, Jefferies does the same thing. This could mean that he is pretending to join her in her lonely meal or, as I would argue, that he has so identified with her that he has begun to copy her actions. If we now take into account the possibility that he is not only identified with Miss Lonely Hearts, but he also is identifying with the invalid wife who is also eating, we can suppose that he is making a double feminine identification. Thus, on a narcissistic and neurotic level, his identification with the other represents a feminine form of identity.

References to the possibility that Jefferies may not be "all man" or that he may identify with the other half of the gender spectrum are constant in the film. When his nurse, Stella, sees that he has been spying on the women outside of his window, she says to him, "You have a hormone deficiency. Those bathing beauties you've been watching haven't raised your temperature one degree in a month." The implication, here, is that Jefferies looks at women but he doesn't get turned on by them.

In another instance, Stella admonishes him for not wanting to marry Lisa. Her argument is that any man with "half a brain" and who can keep "one eye open" would want to marry her right away. Since, Jefferies does not want to do this, we can assume that he has less than half of a brain and less than one eye open. This reference to Jefferies being less than a whole man is only one of a series of comments that put his masculine anatomy in question. When Jefferies is first talking to his boss, he says to him, "I get myself half killed for you." Since his cast is only on the lower part of his body, we don't have to ask what half he has lost.

In another scene, where Lisa is kissing him, Jefferies becomes distracted and starts to look away from her. This irritates her and she exclaims, "When I want a man, I want all of him." Lisa seems to be aware, here, that all of his desire is not directed towards her. Jefferies response to her demand for more attention is to say that, "something is terribly wrong here" and Lisa immediately blames herself.

Here, we find an interesting intersection between our study of feminine sexuality and our analysis of homoerotic desire. The female subject, who is in love with the divided male subject, believes that she is inadequate because she cannot please all of her man. Whereas, the male lover, often responds to his female lover's lesbian desire with a desire to turn her around and to save her from homosexuality, the female lover blames herself for her lover's homosexuality. Both positions deny the fundamental bisexuality of every subject's desire.

The Loss of Sexual Difference

In one of the final scenes, Jefferies' desire for Lisa seems to increase. Part of this change in his position can be related to the fact that Lisa starts to believe his theory of murder, but even more so I would argue that she begins to gain his attention by taking on a more masculine role. In this scene, she has decided to spend the night with him. For the first time in the film, she has her hair up, she is wearing a hat, and she has on a business suit. Up to this point, her hair was always down and she wore large flowing dresses. Lisa's transition to a more masculine way of dressing is coupled with her offer to trade her "feminine intuition" for a bed. In this equation, she is telling Jefferies that if he lets her sleep with him, she will give him her femininity and thus she will be less feminine and he will be more so.

Surrounding this de-feminization of Lisa is a discourse on the difference between private lives and public knowledge. Jefferies' detective friend points out that, "People do a lot of things in private, that they couldn't possibly explain in public." Perhaps this is a reference to Jefferies own closeted sexuality. His desire is private and so he cannot speak about it to others.

When we are trying to decode a hidden form of sexuality, we can always look like we are jumping to conclusions, yet there are certain elements that can only be explained in this film by positing a theory of sexuality that is not simply based along the lines of the active-male-heterosexual-voyeur watches a passive-female-heterosexual-exhibitionist.[11] More so, all of the different references to Jefferies' impotence and anatomical lacks are doubled with his need to find a substitute implement or object of desire. In the film, we see Jefferies place a large, long telephoto lens between his legs. This "telephallus" will be used to look at the killer. In other words, he does not use it to spy on the different women at the apartment complex, but he takes out this substitute organ when he wants to get a closer look at a certain man. While he cannot establish a physical relationship with Thorwald, he attempts to create a bond with him on a visual level.

The other scene where Jefferies places a long phallic object between his legs is at the end of the film, when he takes out his camera flash. This scene is itself surrounded by a feeling of impotence and helplessness. First he sees Lisa in the killer's apartment and there is nothing that he can do. Then the killer enters Jefferies' own apartment and L. B. J. has no way of defending himself, except to use his camera flash as a weapon. This tool of representation is now used to induce blindness, just as his own phallic object only increases his sense of impotency. In this instance, the substitute phallus or fetish does not block the awareness of castration, but rather renders it even more visible.

When the killer approaches him, with the light shining off of his glasses, he first asks Jefferies, "What do you want from me?" This question implies that Jefferies pursuit is about desire—not only what the Other wants of Jefferies, but what Jefferies wants from the Other. In front of this question, Jefferies can only stay silent and attempt to blind the Other. He is not yet ready to come out and speak about his true desire. The voyeur, who is suppose to be the one who sees, is now the one who blinds.

Thus, at the end of the film, we do not have, as Mulvey would suggest, a female character being placed in the position of the castrated object and the male figure being the one who defends against this castration (35). Rather, what we see at the end (our own rear view look) is Jefferies with two broken legs, and Lisa, wearing pants and reading an adventure book. She has become more "masculine," and he is now doubly castrated.[12]

This double castration would seem to problematize the structure of fetishism that Mulvey would like to insist upon.

If the gaze is indeed a form of castration, what we have in the final scene of the film is a triple level of lack that is not covered by any fetishistic image. Jefferies is castrated because he has lost the usage and sight of several of his sexual organs. He is also emasculated, because he cannot see what he wants to see, nor desire what he wants to desire. In turn, Lisa has been masculinized so that she no longer poses a threat to Jefferies' desire. What has help to instigate all of these reversals of roles is the encounter with the gaze of the Other from the position of true desire.

For just a brief moment, Jefferies was face-to-face with the true object that causes his desire. His response to this was to block his and his object's vision, just as Hitchcock has blocked the representation of the scene of homosexuality. Voyeurism is thus indeed the theme of *Rear Window*, but what is given to be seen is not actually what most critics have been looking at. Fascinated by the presence of Grace, they have missed the hairy athlete who hides behind the curtain.

In order to look beyond the fetishistic representation of heterosexual desire, critics and viewers need to pay special attention to the way that the visual level of films often acts as a counter-text to the manifest level of the film's dialogue and narrative plot. In Hitchcock's works, we often find the representation of a straight heterosexual narrative that is coupled with a visual bi-textual discourse. Linked to this bi-textuality is the recognition that every subject of the unconscious finds themselves lacking in relation to the dominant Symbolic order.

In the next chapter, I will analyze *The Birds* in relation to Hitchcock's attempt to dis-engender the traumatic aspects of the Real. This film will help us to see how the visual disruption of the Symbolic order is often coupled with an aural fragmentation that motivates subjects to overcome their sense of loss and lack by forming different systems of ideological closure.

8

The Birds: Zizek, Ideology, and The Horror of the Real

Hitchcock's *The Birds* offers us the opportunity to examine the ways that the bi-textual Real is constantly being gendered female by viewers and critics. Throughout this film, it is impossible to determine whether the attacking birds represent the externalization of the male fear of feminine sexuality or whether these threatening beings represent the masculine death drive. Furthermore, the synthetic quality of the bird's aural invasion renders problematic any quick equation between these created creatures and the natural realm. The birds in this sense represent both the horror of the unstructured Real and the fear of a Symbolically produced form of bi-textual difference.

As I have argued in other chapters, this distinction between the original state of an unsymbolized Real and the produced state of a bi-textual unconscious discourse is crucial to understanding Lacan's theories of ethics and sexuality. Since the Real is by definition impossible to Symbolize, we only have access to this state of natural existence through the return of repressed bi-textual elements. However, the dis-orientation that is caused by the presence of bi-textuality motivates cultures and subjects to find ideological ways to block the reemergence of these destabilizing forces. As we have seen, the male-dominated heterosexual paradigm is one of the crucial mechanisms of ideological interpretation that helps to keep bi-textual desires from reemerging in cultural productions.

An example of the way that the unstructured Real becomes gendered female can be found in Margaret Horowitz's essay *"The Birds:* A Mother's Love."[1] Horowitz argues that the attacks by the birds represent the hero's mother's desire to punish the heroine for desiring her son (279). By equating the attacking birds with the mother's desire to punish, this critic participates in the gendering of these creatures and the formation of a heterosexual Oedipal paradigm. However, I would like to argue that from the very first scene of this film, the question of the gender of these birds is posed and it is continuously posed throughout the rest of the film.

When Melanie Daniels (Tippi Hedren) first attempts to buy a bird, she asks the clerk: "This one won't be a chick, will he?" The film thus begins by raising the problem of gender and sexual identification. This aspect of gender confusion is repeated when Melanie gives a pair of love birds to Mitch Brenner's (Rod Taylor) sister Cathy, who later asks Melanie: "Is there a man and a woman? I can't tell which is which." This undecidability concerning the birds' sexual identification can be, in turn, linked to the horror that people will demonstrate in front of the attacking birds. Furthermore, the fear of sexual dis-orientation in the film is doubled by the critics who constantly need to en-gender the presence of the birds.

Zizek and the Object of Ideology

Another example of this equation of the birds with the attacking mother figure can be found in Slavoj Zizek's book *Looking Awry.*[2] In Zizek's analysis of this film, he stresses the way that the birds represent a "maternal super-ego," which serves to subvert the rule of the Symbolic name-of-the-father (97). While I would not argue with Zizek's point that the birds serve to disrupt and destroy the Symbolic structure, I want to examine the equation of the birds with the maternal super-ego and the way that this reading could be seen as an ideological attempt to force the unsymbolizable Real into a gendered position. Moreover, I want to explore the way that the three alternative readings of this film that Zizek locates in Robin Wood's chapter on The Birds represent three different ways of ideologically projecting the horror of the Real into the place of the Other.[3]

The first possible reading of this film, and in fact all of Hitchcock's films, is what Zizek calls the "cosmological" interpretation (97). This argument is based on the idea that Hitchcock is primarily a thinker who is profoundly influenced by a certain theological perspective that stresses the arbitrariness of an "impenetrable God" (97). In other words, the birds represent the pure irrationality of a dark God that rules the world through blind randomness and chance. This randomness of the Other is then played out in Hitchcock's films through a series of chance encounters and falsely accused innocent men.

What this "cosmological" theory fails to take into account is the way that God becomes a projection for all of the Real objects that cannot be represented in the Symbolic. Thus, God is everywhere, but cannot be seen or represented directly, either in word or in image. In strictly Freudian terms, we can say that God represents the Imaginary idealization of the Symbolic father. Yet, in Zizek's reading, the Symbolic father has been replaced by the engulfing maternal figure who prevents the subject from having a "normal" sexual relation (99). The ideological displacement and projection here is from the evil God to the evil mother.

Zizek insists that what the birds represent is some fundamental discord in the intersubjective structure of the family (99). To be more precise, he posits that "the dead end *The Birds* is really about is, of course, that of the modern American family: the deficient paternal ego-ideal makes the law "regress" towards a ferocious maternal super-ego, affecting sexual enjoyment—the decisive trait of the libidinal structure of 'pathological narcissism'"(99). This historical and diagnostic reading is as ideological as it is insightful, for it allows us to see how the dread of the Real gets projected onto a dread of the feminine, this time in the guise of the mother as the engulfing bird.

The second possible reading that Zizek discusses is the "ecological" interpretation, which would seem to go along with Lacan's theory about the way that the Symbolic order negates and destroys the Real and the way that the subject of the unconscious resists this form of Symbolic destruction. Zizek affirms that from this perspective, the birds represent the revenge of the exploited natural realm. However, in his humorous reworking of the title of the film as "Birds of the World, Unite," Zizek points to the way that this reading projects onto the environment, in an anthropomorphic way, the role of being the exploited working class (97). The birds here become the workers of the Communist Manifesto, who must unite together in order to throw off the shackles of exploitive capitalism. What is in part behind this transformation of the natural birds into a collective political movement is the attempt to posit in the last resort some level of intentionality and purpose in the place of the unintentional and therefore un-conscious Real. The horror of the randomness of nature is thus displaced and transformed into the horror of some organized political movement. Furthermore, this reading exposes the way that class anxieties and the fear of social change may be related to a fundamental anxiety concerning the unknowability of other people's intentions.

The third reading that is offered by Wood and Zizek is the "familial" analysis that we have already begun to discuss. Here, the birds no longer represent an evil God or a collective natural force, but rather the main character's overly involved mother (98). In this reading, it is the absence of the Symbolic father that allows for the emergence of the all-powerful primitive mother.

Later on in his book, Zizek posits a fourth reading of *The Birds*, which I believe goes beyond the other three forms of interpretation. He argues that "the birds do not 'signify' the maternal super-ego, they do not 'symbolize' blocked sexual relations, the 'possessive mother' and so on" (104). In other words, Zizek is here working against the equation of the birds with the maternal super-ego. In fact, as his text continues, we find out that he now posits that the birds "are, rather, the making present in the real, the objectivization, the incarnation of the fact that, on the symbolizing level, something 'has not worked out,' in short the objectivization-positivization of a failed symbolization" (104). From this

angle, the birds fundamentally portray a failure of representation that allows for making present in the Real a lack in
the Symbolic order. This is not to say that Hitchcock
attempts to return to the Real itself, but rather that he
stresses the way that the subject represents a hole in the
Symbolic structure.

Zizek's reading thus places at the center of the historical and psychological forms of interpretation, a consideration
of the relationship between the Symbolic and the Real. This
important move forces us to search for a linguistic cause that
would help us to determine the forces of social history and
family narratives. In this sense, problems of representation
must supersede considerations of psychological and social
history.

Re-reading the Birds

In order to follow Zizek's lead in reading this film, I
would like to first concentrate on the connection between the
invasion of the birds and the destruction of the Symbolic
order. In fact, one does not have to look very far in order to
see this connection because in the very beginning of the film,
during the opening credits, the birds are shown attacking
and destroying the names of the people in the film. Of
course, the last name to be eaten up by the birds is
Hitchcock's own name. In other words, before the film even
begins, there is a dismantling of the Symbolic Name-of-the-
Father and an encounter with the nothingness of the authorial subject himself.

Matching this attack on the Symbolic order is the birds'
preference for attacking the eyes of its victims. The first
casualty that we find in the film is a farmer who has had his
eyes eaten out by the birds. When Mitch's mother Lydia
finds this man, the absence of his eyes is matched by the
image of her mouth open wide in horror showing just a black
hole. Here, the loss of masculine sight and vision is matched
with the feminine loss of voice and the gaping hole of the
subject. These bodily holes and absences represent the blockage of representation, both visual and aural, by the invasion

of the birds and they serve to highlight the subject who is only a hole in the Symbolic order.

In one of the next scenes, we watch a slow build-up of the birds outside of the school building, while the students inside repetitively sing a meaningless song. Once again, I would argue that the failure of language to represent or convey meaning (the meaningless, repetitive song) is matched with the growing presence of the birds. In this sense, the sounds and presence of the birds represent a language which has lost its ability to communicate or convey meaning.[4]

When the birds do finally attack the children, we see on the ground a pair of shattered glasses. The fact that the camera focuses on these broken tools of vision serves to reinforce the way that the birds stand in for the nothingness that is the other side of consciousness and vision. Consciousness, as I have argued, is most often attached to some level of visual control and intentionality.[5] What the birds then represent is precisely that which has no vision or intentionality. No one knows why the birds attack, just as the viewer might wonder why the main character Melanie does what she does. Perhaps one of the points of the film is to present this unintentional element that forces everyone to come up with some explanation that will serve to hold at bay the possibility that in the Real there is no intentionality or reason. We shall see that the way that people react to this eruption of the Real in the film is by employing certain heterosexist and xenophobic ideological formations.

In the scene where Melanie is talking on the phone to her father about the recent bird attack, everyone in the restaurant starts to come up with different theories in order to explain the strange actions of the birds. The drunk at the end of the bar, takes a theological position and insists that the attack of the birds represents the end of the world. Another person at the bar is a bird expert, who attempts to explain away the attack in scientific terms, while someone else is influenced by a militaristic ideology and claims that the birds represent an "attack on humanity." Finally, the bird specialist claims that birds of different species never flock together, and if they did, that would be the end. This final theory for the birds seems to be one based on the need for racial segregation.

No matter what these different theories are and how well they match the different theories that Zizek has discussed, I believe their sheer proliferation points to the desperate attempts that people make in order to explain away any action that doesn't seem to follow any strict causal logic.[6] At the end of the film, the audience's response is often the exasperated repeated question of why the birds attacked in the first place.

All of the explanations that we can give to this question can only be ideological responses that attempt to project onto the place of the Other, a fundamental experience of nothingness. In order to hide the unknowability of the birds' intentions people blame God, their neighbors, Melanie's erotic desire, and the threat of miscegenation. The film itself continuously attempts, and ultimately fails, to account for the attack of the birds. This does not mean that there is no value in us trying to read this film; rather, we must change our focus and examine the different Imaginary constructions that are structured around the central lack of the film. For it is these Imaginary constructions that constitute the ideological level of this text.[7]

The first ideology that is elaborated in the film is what I will call the "ideology of love." Upon first meeting Melanie, Mitch consciously equates her with a bird by saying, "Back in your cage Melanie Daniels." Of course, Mitch is in the pet shop himself in order to buy some "love birds." Through a process of substitution it is not a leap to say that Mitch would like to cage Melanie, in order to make her his lover and to be more exact, in order to get her to submit to his law. This attempt to control the Other through love is a major way that a subject can turn his or her encounter with a lack of being into a positive experience. As a totalized object of love and beauty, Melanie represents an Imaginary form of wholeness for the lacking masculine subject; if Mitch can idealize her, he can then identify with the object of his idealization. In fact this identification between Mitch and Melanie is signaled at the end of the film when Mitch plays the role of the bird instead of Melanie. This transition becomes evident when after Melanie is attacked by the birds the last time, Mitch tries to approach her and she swats him away as if she is swatting the birds. Of course, these birds have now moved from the position of being love birds to being attack birds.

This movement from love to hate in the film is doubled by the transformation of sexuality into punishment. In the first scene of the film, we see Melanie walking down the street, and then we hear what we assume to be a man whistling at her. In response to this whistle, she turns around and smiles, only to see birds, and not a desiring man, chirping at her. In this scene, the masculine mating call or whistle, which she responds to in a favorable show of desire, is then followed by a threat from the position of the birds.

In another scene, when Melanie first approaches Mitch's house and the camera takes on her subjective angle, her pursuit of love and her control of vision are followed by the first attack of a bird. This scene can be read as reinforcing Tania Modleski's argument that women in Hitchcock's films are punished when they explicitly show desire or visual control.[8] In the case of *The Birds*, love turns into hatred the moment that the passive object of desire attempts to take on an active subjective position.

According to Modleski, another reason why women have to be castrated or punished in film is so that men can repress or deny their own feminine identifications. Modleski continues by positing that Hitchcock often overidentifies with the female characters in his films and the result of this is a potential loss of authorial control (60). In many ways, *The Birds* substantiates this argument. I would like to posit that in most of Hitchcock's films there is indeed an identification between the director and a woman in the film who represents the one who knows and sees. Most often this connection is made by the female subject wearing eyeglasses. In the case of *The Birds*, the Annie Hayworth character (the school teacher, i.e. the guardian of knowledge) plays this role, and Hitchcock's identification with her is heightened by the fact that they share the same initials—A. H.

If I am correct in making this identification between Hitchcock and the school teacher, I must add that near the end of the film, Annie also has her eyes eaten out, just as we might argue that Hitchcock loses his own visual control through the arbitrary nature of the birds and his own inability to control the laws of representation. Thus, Hitchcock himself becomes the gaze which sees nothing, but which stares out at us through the gaping holes of an eyeless face.

A Reversal of Fantasy

This gaze reduced to a look of nothingness brings us back to Zizek's own theorization of the Lacanian object and its role in ideology, fantasy, and symptom formation. We may say that Hitchcock's fundamental fantasy is structured by a scene where he is reduced to being a pure passive gaze that is stared at by a desiring Other. However, on the level of his Imaginary fantasy, this structure is reversed and he becomes the looking subject that places the object of representation within a certain frame and upon a directed screen.[9]

Following Zizek's work, we must distinguish between two opposed structures of fantasy. On the level of the fundamental fantasy, we are always dealing with what Zizek calls "the hard kernel of the real" that resists all attempts at symbolization.[10] However, on the level of the Imaginary fantasy, the object itself is symbolized and taken up in a structure of Imaginary representation. "It is precisely the role of fantasy to give the coordinates of the subject's desire, to specify the object, to locate the position the subject assumes in it."[11] This "specification" of the object occurs through its scenic representation, where the blank screen of nothingness is filled with the different images of wish-fulfillment.

In *Looking Awry*, Zizek explains this process where the undefinable object takes on a determined form and definition:

The paradox of desire is that it posits retroactively its own cause, i.e., the object (*a*) is an object that can be perceived only by a gaze "distorted" by desire, an object that does not exist for an "objective" gaze. In other words, the object (*a*) is always, by definition, perceived in a distorted way, because outside this distortion, in itself, "it does not exist," since it is nothing but the embodiment, the materialization of this very distortion (12).

This transformation of the object of nothingness into an object of desire helps to elucidate the movement from the confusion caused by a primal scene of gender ambiguity towards the implication of the object into a heterosexual paradigm.

Zizek's own criticism articulates together these two opposing forces of ideological identification and Real bi-textuality. On the one hand, he accounts for the social construction of different ideological formations, while on the other hand, he depicts the return of the unsymbolized Real. This double strategy produces a paradoxical structure that matches Hitchcock's own work. For Hitchcock is a producer of ideologically mass-consumed movies, as well as artistic meditations on the limits of all forms of representation. Like Melanie Daniels in *The Birds*, Hitchcock moves from being caged in the structure of the Other to being a separated material object that people can not control or contain in their fields of knowledge and vision.

In agreement with Zizek, I would argue that the object (*a*) is the only true something that we have and that this core of our presence and identity is what desire in the structure of an Imaginary fantasy constantly attempts to circumvent. In the case of *The Birds*, we can say that the staring empty gaze of the subject, as well as the meaningless attacks and sounds of the birds, represents our true presence in the world divorce from any level of Imaginary intentionality and Symbolic definition. What still remains uncertain is what type of analysis and political activity can grow out of such an awareness of the material foundations of our identity.

Zizek's reading of Lacan allows us to see how the innermost core of our being rejects all forms of Symbolization. Yet, Lacan does develop a theory of agency that is based on the materiality of the letter and not on Imaginary fantasy or Symbolic mastery. In his theory of the discourse of the analyst, Lacan places the object (*a*) in the position of the agent that causes the emergence of unconscious desire and a production and loss of subjective identifications:

$$\text{(agent) } \underline{a} \text{ ----------> } \underline{\$} \text{ (desiring subject)}$$
$$\text{(knowledge) } \overline{S2} \qquad \overline{S1} \text{ (identification)}$$

This new definition of political agency would stress the role of emerging desire, multiple and shifting identifications, the recognition that knowledge is never complete and that truth can only be half-said. Likewise, by calling into question the totality of knowledge and truth by privileging the unsymbolized aspects of the Real, this form of agency would counter all attempts at ideological projection and closure.

Perhaps the place to start in the formation of this new political agency is in the very act of teaching and reading itself. This would entail a new form of pedagogy that allows for the play of identifications, the putting into question of all forms of knowledge, and the criticism of different attempts at ideological control and reduction. By reading such texts as *The Birds* against their ideological interpretations, we can begin to expose the ideological structure of projection, while we allow for the emergence of alternative forms of desire and identification.

Epilogue

Psycho and the Horror of the Bi-Textual Unconscious

Throughout this work, I have focused on the relationship between Lacanian psychoanalysis, feminist theories,
and Queer Theory. In this interaction, we have learned that
many feminist and psychoanalytic concepts and structures
depend upon a heterosexist model of sexual difference that
equates masculinity with the Symbolic order and feminity
with the Real. The result of this process is that the unconscious becomes "heterosexualized." I have countered this het-
errosexual logic by developing the theory of bi-textuality.

This notion of a polyvalent foundation of sexuality and
textuality is derived directly from Freud's early theory that
the unconscious is inherently bi-sexual. In one of the most
crucial passages in the *Three Essays on the Theory of
Sexuality*, Freud argues that heterosexuality, and not homosexuality, is the form of desire that has to be constructed and
explained: "All human beings are capable of making a homosexual object-choice and have in fact made one in their
unconscious. . . . Thus from the point of view of psychoanalysis the exclusive sexual interest felt by men for women is
also a problem that needs elucidating and is not a self-evi-
dent fact."[1] Due to America's cultural homophobia, this foundational argument by Freud has been repressed and thus a
major part of his theory has been neglected.

One reason why the homosexual and bi-sexual aspects
of the unconscious have been ignored is due to the dis-orienting aspects of bi-textual desire. Multiple forms of sexuality

135

and textuality upset the clear binary logic of sexual difference. The bi-textuality of the unconscious also threatens the
heterosexual control of the Symbolic order. Our culture is
therefore grounded on the repression of the unconscious and
the need to avoid any encounter with the Real of bi-sexuality.
In Hitchcock's *Psycho*, this horror of the Real and the bi-textual becomes associated with the fear of psychosis.

I would like to argue that *Psycho* represents Hitchcock's
own retrospective look back at his previous films and an
anticipation of some future movies. I will argue that almost
every scene and symbol in this film either directly cites or
plays off of another scene or symbol from an earlier film. The
central films and themes that I have been discussing
throughout this book can be summarized in the following
list: the effaced female subject (*The Lady Vanishes*), the masculine horror of the feminine (*Spellbound*), repetition and
the Real (*Rebecca*), feminine fluidity and be-hind sight
(*Notorious*), internalized abjection (*Marnie*), sublimation and
melancholia (*Vertigo*), homoerotism and the gaze (*Rear
Window*), and the maternal super-ego (*The Birds*). I would
like to posit that *Psycho* circulates these different images
and themes in a postmodern way that renders all questions
of temporality and intentionality problematic. More so, the
bi-textual themes and impulses, which Hitchcock merely
Symbolizes or hints at in his other works, are projected out
into the Real during this film.[2]

The Structure of Psychosis

This need to represent Symbolic attributes in the Real
can be, in part, explained by the central focus of the film,
which is Norman Bates' psychosis. As Lacan has often
pointed out, one of the major defining characteristics of psychosis is that certain Symbolic relations and concepts, that
are "normally" abstract factors of structure and order,
become perceived in the Real during psychotic states.[3] In the
case of *Psycho*, the subject's Symbolic desire to identify with
his mother will be acted out on the level of the Real, when he
actually attempts to take on his mother's voice and clothing.

Another defining characteristic of psychosis is the rejection of the subject's super-ego and its externalization into the Real. Freud points out that all of us have a conscience, or what Lacan would call an "internalized Other," that listens to our thoughts and judges our desires. However, what happens in psychosis is that the subject actually perceives in the Real, the Other listening to his or her thoughts and desires.[4] Delusions of observation, as well as paranoia, can thus be explained by the externalization of the internalized Other.

If Norman Bates becomes his mother at the end of the film, it is, in part, because he has so identified with her law and desires after her death that he cannot separate his self from her conscience. Likewise, in the scenes where we believe that we hear his mother yelling at Norman, what is actually going on is that he has projected his own conscience outside of himself and he is now yelling at himself from the position of the (m)Other. We must read this film, therefore, on the level of a long extended psychotic delusion that forces all of Hitchcock's more subtle themes out into the open.

One way that the structure of this film has been read is by dividing it into three sections: the first section concerns the sexuality and criminality of the female subject, Marion Crane; the next section switches focus and is more concerned with the desire and fears of the masculine subject, Norman Bates; and the final section deals with the social search for the missing woman and the assumption by Norman Bates of his mother's voice and identity. According to Barbara Klinger, this three-part structure centers on a dialectical discussion of feminine sexuality, "The narrative of *Psycho* can be seen to function in its movement to present this problem [feminine sexuality], to repress it (the switch in narratives) and restate it (Norman-the mother), and finality to contain/solve it in the name of the family and the law."[5] In this structure, the problem of sexual difference is, in part, resolved through the psychotic resolution of the film. However, I would like to argue that what this film presents is a radically ambivalent representation of feminine sexuality that does not fit into any type of dialectical resolution, but rather serves to materialize a radical splitting of the female subject through the emergence of bi-textual desire.

From the opening credits of *Psycho*, this projection of the split subject is evident. When we first see the names and the titles of the film appear, each name is sliced into sections. Hitchcock will later reuse this method in *The Birds*, when he shows the titles being eaten away. Of course Hitchcock's own name is shown to be divided, reunited, and then split again, and I believe we can read this as an indication of his identification with the divided female subject.

One may initially respond to my stress on the female subject in this film by claiming that the central focus is on Norman Bates, who is a male figure that finally gets united with his Other half at the end of the movie. Thus, it would seem that *Psycho* is not about feminine sexuality and division, but rather concerns masculinity and the desire to reunite with the lost maternal love-object. In fact, I would not argue with this second interpretation, and I would add that these two different readings represent two sides of the same coin. In other words, the male subject's desire to reunite himself with his other half demands that the female object be split and divided.

In order to demonstrate this latter theory, I will read the film backwards, starting with the long psychiatric explanation for Norman's behavior. According to the court appointed psychiatrist, Norman's mind was divided between himself and the voice of his mother. We can read the name "Norman" as a condensation of the "normal man." What is normal, then, is for the male subject to be divided in half between his identifications with his mother and her desire and his identification with his father. Freud's theory of the universal bisexuality points to this fundamental subjective division that remains repressed in the unconscious for most subjects. However, what happens in psychosis is this unconscious bi-textual split is experienced as a Real perception.

In Norman's case, every time he has a masculine desire his mother's voice reacts against it. We can suppose that for most subjects this battle between desire and the voice of conscience goes on internally, but with Norman we actually hear his debate with his conscience out loud. The psychiatrist explains that the origin of Norman's psychosis occurred after he killed his mother and her lover. As in the case of a psychotic process of mourning, Norman identified with his lost object and took on his mother's identity. The transitive nature of this relationship is expressed when the psychiatrist points out that because Norman was so jealous of his mother, he assumed that she was so jealous of him. Thus, when Norman met Marion and he became attracted to her, his mother's jealousy, or rather the projection of his own jealousy, called for Marion's murder. He then had to erase all of the traces of the crime, just as he erased all of the traces of his mother's death, in order to keep up the illusion that she was still alive. More over, to hold onto the presence of his mother in the Real, he kept her body in her bedroom.

The male's need to keep the female subject in the Real, which is so evident in Hitchcock's other films, is taken here to its logical extreme. The female body is transformed into a corpse that is now truly outside of the Symbolic order of law and discourse; this body remains a gaze or a dead stare that cannot be effaced by the subject.

This presence of the dead staring gaze is manifested in one of the last lines of the film, when Norman states through his mother's voice, "As if I could do anything except sit and stare like one of his stuffed birds. They're probably watching me. I'm not even going to swat that fly." The protesting inactivity of this subject, who can only sit and stare, can be related to the effacement of the female subject by the Symbolic order that attempts to pose and manipulate her body.

The final image in the film of a rope pulling a car out of the water echoes this notion of the female subject that has been reduced to being a pure inert object of resistance. For it is Marion's body that is hidden inside the car that has been pushed into the swamp and is now being dredged up. According to Klinger, this last view of the car reflects a process that began with the opening scenes of Marion in a hotel room:

> Marion is transformed in this progression from an overt erotic spectacle (semiclad, in postcoital embrace) to a figure entirely shrouded from view (a body in the trunk of a car): a figure initially manifested strongly as spectacle becomes an almost complete visual nonentity. (334)

The female image, which I have shown is often at the center of Hitchcock's field of representation, has now been reduced to being an absent object. The Lady has once again vanished but this time she will not return.

If the female subject has now been murdered, it is clear that Hitchcock and the process of filmmaking has killed her off. This connection between murder and representation becomes clear in the famous shower scene where each stab at Marion's body is matched with a cut of the film and camera angle. In other terms, the film editor and director are the ones that are cutting up the female body by breaking down her image into separate angles and views. Through the analysis of the ethics of representation, we learn that film feeds on the feminine body, but it can only represent it by cutting and ultimately killing it. Once again, I would argue that Hitchcock has hinted at this before but here he is presenting the ethical connection between murder and representation in the Real; the male-dominated cultural order works by effacing the female subject and pushing her body towards the limits of the representable.

If we now look at the beginning of this movie, we can see that Hitchcock himself returns to one of his earliest films. Just as in the opening of *The Lady Vanishes*, the camera slowly and silently enters through a window and into a room at a cheap hotel. We see Marion partially undressed and laying on a bed while she talks to her lover, Sam. She tells him that this will be their last time together and that she is tired of meeting secretively.

Sex as a secret is a common theme in Hitchcock's work; yet, in this film, the female body is presented in a more explicit way than in most of his other films. Rarely in a Hitchcock picture, do we see a female character so undressed and perhaps the most revealing scene in all of his work up to this point is the shower scene, which results in such a violent reaction. One could argue that Hitchcock's ability to create an atmosphere of suspense is dependent on his strong desire to repress his own sexual and violent urges. However, in this film, everything is pushed up a notch, and that which is usually concealed begins to be revealed. This movement of revelation is, in part, highlighted when Sam says to Marion:

"You make respectability seem disrespectful." Hitchcock's attempt to present sexuality in a respectful way has now crossed over to its crude opposite.

In the second scene of the film, this movement from concealed desire to overt representation occurs on the level of money. At the bank where Marion works, a wealthy client, Mr. Cassidy, can't help but to wave his $40,000 in front of everyone's faces as he flirts with Marion. She seems to ignore his passes; however, once she is intrusted with his money, she decides to take it for herself. We then see her return to a room where she changes clothing, and is now presented in black lingerie instead of white. This section of the film will be later repeated in *Marnie* where we find another female character who steals from her boss and whose name also starts off with the letters "Mar."[6]

In fact, the similarities do not stop here because Marnie also changes colors and names like Marion. While Marnie changes her name to Mary, Marion, and Martha; Marion changes her name to Marie Samuels. The stress on the "mar" in all of these names points to the marring effect that representation has on women. Although, in *Psycho* the female subject will not only be marred on a Symbolic level, but she will be effaced in the Real.

This marring effect of language on the feminine body is doubled in the film by the connection between money and sexuality. In the first scene at the hotel, Marion stresses to Sam that she also pays for their secret affair. Then in the next scene at the bank, the flirting man proposes to buy her love. After she steals his money, so that in part he cannot do this, she hears his voice in her head saying, "If anything is missing, I'll replace it with her fine smooth flesh." As Lacan has argued, the signifier attaches itself to the body by removing a pound of flesh.[7] Here, the process of signification is tied directly to the commodification of the female body. She has stolen money from him, so he feels that he is entitled to some of her flesh—it is not only the name that demands to become flesh but it is also the almighty dollar.

Furthermore, the dollar as an object of exchange doubles the presence of the female object as an object of circulation in the masculine economy. Once, Marion steals the money, she then upsets these two circuits of exchange. Hitchcock highlights the way that this object is the material residue of all Symbolic exchanges by having the letter full of money always sticking out of Marion's purse. Like the object (*a*), this part of the Real that has been submitted to the Symbolic order refuses to be completely negated. The protruding envelope points to the final image of the protruding car trunk that hides the remains of the negated female body.

When Marion finally does pull into the Bates Hotel, her approach to the large house in the rain recalls the second Mrs. de Winter's approach to Manderley in *Rebecca*. Both homes loom large and are filled with the presence of a murdered female/maternal figure. Like Norman, Max in *Rebecca* has killed a woman and has placed her in a vehicle that is now submerged under water. And like the reemergence of Rebecca's body from the sea, Marion's body will reemerge at the end of *Psycho*.

The Real(m) of the Birds

Once Marion is inside Norman's parlor, we see that he is quite obsessed by birds. In a room that is filled with stuffed birds, he says to Marion, whose real last name is Crane, that she eats like a bird. All of these references point to the association between his mother and the birds, which becomes explicit at the end of the film. Marion is thus placed in the same position as his mother; she must be contained by being stuffed and reduced to being a pure, dead stare.

Of course, these references to birds anticipate the movie that Hitchcock will later make, which has this animal as its central figure. If the bird represents the maternal super-ego as Zizek has argued, than we must ask what does the stuffed bird represent and how does it relate to Norman's attempt to stuff his mother's voice into his own body?[8]

A partial response to this question is provided by Norman's soliloquy on the human condition that he delivers to Marion in his back parlor:

I think we're all in our private traps, clamped in them and none of us can ever get out. We scratch and we claw, but only at the air and at each other, and for all of it, we never budge an inch.

Here, Norman is no longer saying that Marion is like a bird, or that his mother is like one, but rather that all subjects are trapped in cages like birds that are going to be stuffed. But what is this human cage if not the solitude of our own bodies and consciousness? Isn't Hitchcock's point, in this very self-revealing moment, that all connections between people are fundamentally impossible because we are all trapped within our own cages or bodies?

On the other hand, if we are all stuck in our own private hells, that does not mean that other people don't try to place us in other forms and hellish places. When Marion suggests to Norman that he should place his mother "in" a mental institution, he becomes enraged and replies:

Put her in some place! What do you know about caring? Have you ever seen the inside of one of those places? The laughing and the tears, the cruel eyes studying you, my mother there! She's as harmless as one of those stuffed birds.

This resistance of the subject who has identified with his mother is a resistance to being placed within the Symbolic structure of the Other and under the Other's observation. In order to prevent this, he would rather kill her and stuff her like a bird. If we now apply this argument to Hitchcock's own conflicted attempts at reducing and representing female bodies and fluids (*Notorious*) in fixed forms, we see that his desire to control his own horror of the feminine results in a transformation of feminine presence into being a fixed dead object.

Connected to this mortification of the female body, we find the unconscious insistence of letters and writing. After their extended exchange of views on birds and human nature, Marion goes back to her room, but she makes a mistake by using her real name instead of her false one.

Norman then goes back and checks her signature in his guest book and he realizes that she has been lying. This scene repeats in its essence, the scene in *Spellbound*, where Constance compares signatures and discovers that Dr. Edwards is not who he says he is. As in many of Hitchcock's other films, the first sign of guilt and material proof comes in the form of writing. Once again, it is an unconscious slip and the insistence of the letter that provides evidence for the resolution of the mystery.

After Norman makes this discovery, he then goes back into his room, and he removes a picture so that he can watch Marion undress in her room. Here we have a restating of the *Rear Window* theme of voyeurism, which is another film where a woman's body is cut into pieces. Of course, in the first film, we only hear about this murder—it is only reproduced in the Symbolic—but in this version, we actually get to witness it visually.

Before the cutting of the female body occurs in *Psycho*, there is a prefiguring of this event. Marion decides that she is going to return the money she has stolen and she calculates on a piece of paper how much she owes. She then rips up the paper and flushes it down the toilet. The camera focuses on the water and the ripped paper being sucked down into the hole of the toilet. Later, after Marion herself is cut up in the shower, we will see her blood being sucked down into the hole of the bathtub. She is, thus, placed in the same position as the ripped-up letter. In fact, the first clue that her sister will find of her presence at the Bates Hotels will be a piece of this paper that has resisted being flushed.

Later on as we watch Marion's blood spin down the shower drain, we see superimposed an image of her open eye which begins to spin around. This eye recalls the female eye that we see at the beginning of *Vertigo*. This female subject has now been truly reduced to being a dead gaze, which stares, but can no longer see. She is the material residue of the negation of the Real by the Symbolic order. In this sense, she resists being completely absorbed by the system of the Other. It is precisely this resistance of the Real and the feminine subject/object that I have placed at the center of Lacan's theory of ethics. Hitchcock not only shows us the murder of the feminine Thing, but he also forces us to acknowledge this act of Symbolic destruction by having the dead eye of the woman stare at us as her blood runs down the drain.

In order to further instill this image of the blood running into a hole, Hitchcock shows Marion's car, which now holds her dead body, slowly sink into the swamp. As we watch this car begin to submerge, we see a round white circle that slowly disappears into nothingness. This image then recalls the flushing toilet bowl and the shower drain, but now in a reversal of structure, a solid object is being surrounded by water, instead of a solid form sucking in water.

This reversal of the flow of water relates to the theme of feminine fluidity that I have traced in *Notorious*. While, Norman might attempt to mop up all of Marion's feminine fluids, like Lady Macbeth, he will never be able to erase all of the blood from his memory. This horror of the ineffaceable blood becomes evident when we hear Norman yell, "Mother, oh God mother, blood!"[9]

Discourse Around the Missing Object

The next section of the film is started by the private investigator, who says to Sam and Marion's sister, "Let's all talk about Marion." For a great deal of the rest of the film, no one will do anything else, but precisely this—talk about the missing feminine object and attempt to absorb this lack into the Symbolic order of discourse. The role of the investigator is to seek out clues to account for the disappearance of Marion and the money. At one point, he insists that she must be visible because "Someone always sees a girl with $40,000." The idea, here, is that money as a material form of Symbolic circulation makes the absent feminine body present. As in the case of *Rebecca* and *The Lady Vanishes*, the only proof of a woman's existence is the material traces of the Symbolic order. In *Psycho*, the first clue for the investigator is her signature in the guest book. Even though she has signed a different name, the investigator makes the connection by comparing her handwriting.

The second clue that this detective sees is what appears to be a person's face in a window at the big house. When he confronts Norman about this, Norman first denies it and then he admits that it is his mother, but she is an invalid. This spotting of the invalid female in the window is another direct quote from *Rear Window*. And like this previous film, the attempt of the subject to investigate this gaze, by entering into the home of the other, will result in a scene of violent confrontation. However, in the case of *Rear Window*, Lisa survives this encounter, while in *Psycho*, the investigator is brutally murdered.

While Sam and the sister are waiting to hear from the detective, they become suspicious and they go see the Sheriff of the town. They tell him that the investigator said something about seeing Norman's mother at the window. The sheriff replies that this is impossible because Norman's mother has been dead for over ten years and is buried at a cemetery near by. This situation of the buried female body, that is not really buried, is another reference to *Rebecca*, whose body everyone thought was already identified and buried a year before she is rediscovered.

When Marion's sister finally enters the Bates' home, she first becomes convinced that the mother is still alive because she sees a bodily indentation in her bed. While she is exploring the inside of Norman's house, Sam is questioning Norman outside in his office. He confronts Norman and states, "I've been talking about your mother, your motel." In a strange equation, the mother is, here, equated with the hotel; both are empty structures that are filled with vacancy.

Right after this exchange between Sam and Norman, we see Marion's sister discover Norman's mother in the basement. As she slowly turns a chair around, we begin to view the mother's dead skeleton and staring, empty eye sockets. This empty gaze, the look without vision, refers back to the relation between the mother and the empty, vacant hotel. The maternal body is only a shell, a place of enclosure that is filled with nothingness. When Norman then attempts to identify with his mother in the Real by taking on her voice, he is, in part, trying to reoccupy and reanimate her body. This return to the maternal body and the attempt to give it a voice represents the movement of Hitchcock's work itself. In order to materialize the absent Real of the female body, he can only reenact its destruction and attempt to let it speak through him.

I have been calling this return of the repressed female subject an "ethical" relationship because it allows us to see the way that our systems of representation work by killing off the Real of human existence. At the end of the film, we have the situation where a murdered female voice is communicating through a possessed male body. This structure represents a reversal of the classical filmic relationship between the masculine voice and the female form. Instead of the male character telling the female body where to go and what to do, we have the invasion of a female voice within a masculine form. The result of this process is a highlighting of the bisexual and divided nature of every human subject.

Through the discourse of psychosis, Hitchcock is now able to bring out into the open his own cross-gendered identifications. The voice of this subject has become the bi-textual voice of the unconscious that calls out of the void and articulates the ethical demand for a return to the Real. Furthermore, Norman's bi-textual psychosis subverts the feminist en-gendering of the Real by highlighting the cultural horror of bisexual desire and unconscious discourse. From this perspective, we can read *Psycho* as the projection of Hitchcock's most profound cultural fears and desires.

This horror of the bi-textual Real that surfaces in *Psycho* points to one of the main mechanisms of control that the dominant heterosexist Symbolic order employs in order to contain and silence diverse forms of desire and identification. In order to work against this process of containment and repression, cultural workers need to explore the ways that the unconscious and the Real become equated with feminine and queer subjects. Linked to this process of exposing the en-gendering of the Real is an awareness of the ways that Symbolic castration is rejected and projected onto debased Others. Hitchcock's work has offered us the opportunity to view the ways that bi-textuality challenges and subverts the imposition of the death drive and the Symbolic order of law and sexual regulation.

Notes

Introduction

1. This connection between feminine subjectivity and writing is essential in the work of Hélène Cixous, Julia Kristeva, and Luce Irigaray. For a general introduction to this topic, see Elaine Showalter, "Feminist Criticism in the Wilderness," in *Modern Criticism and Theory* edited by David Lodge (New York: Longman House, 1991), pp. 331–353.

2. Lacan's seminar *Encore* often relates writing to femininity. Part of this seminar has been translated into English and can be found in *Feminine Sexuality*, translated by Jacqueline Rose (New York: W. W. Norton, 1982), pp. 138–161.

3. Judith Butler, *Bodies That Matter* (New York: Routledge, 1993).

4. See Luce Irigaray, "The Mechanics of Solids," in *The Sex Which Is Not One*, translated by Catherine Porter with Carolyn Burke (Ithaca: Cornell Univ. Press, 1985), pp. 106–118.

5. Laura Mulvey, "Visual Pleasure and Narrative Cinema," in *Issues in Feminist Film Criticism*, edited by Patricia Erens (Bloomington: Indiana Univ. Press, 1990), pp. 28–40.

6. Slavoj Zizek, *Looking Awry* (Cambridge: MIT Press, 1992), pp. 96–99.

7. This notion of the blockage of unconscious representations is developed in the section "The Hitchcockian Blot," in Zizek's *Looking Awry*.

149

8. Kaja Silverman, *The Acoustic Mirror* (Bloomington: Indiana Univ. Press, 1988). This book offers an extended analysis of this dialectic between the female body and the male voice.

9. Tania Modleski, *The Women Who Knew Too Much* (New York: Routledge, 1988) often returns to the idea of a bisexual reading of Hitchcock's identifications and desires, yet she doesn't pursue this theme as a central topic.

10. See Kaja Silverman, *Male Subjectivity at the Margins* (New York: Routledge, 1992).

11. The inspiration for this concept of "female homosocial desire" comes from Eve Kosofsky Sedgwick, *Between Men: English Literature and Male Homosocial Desire* (New York: Columbia Univ. Press, 1985).

12. For a discussion of Lacan's interpretation of Freud's theory of the death drive, see Robert Samuels, *Between Philosophy and Psychoanalysis* (New York: Routledge Press, 1983), pp. 33–34, 120–121, 151 n.3 and n.4.

13. Jacques Lacan, *The Seminar of Jacques Lacan: Book VII The Ethics of Psychoanalysis 1959–1960*, edited by Jacques-Alain Miller, and translated by Dennis Porter (New York: Routledge, 1992).

14. Two recent attempts at reading Lacan's Ethics seminar can be found in John Rajchman, *Truth and Eros* (New York: Routledge, 1991), and Tobin Siebers, *The Ethics of Criticism* (Ithaca: Cornell Univ. Press, 1988). I believe that because both Rajchman and Siebers miss the radical nature of Lacan's theory of the death drive, they misconstrue Lacan's ethical theory.

15. It would be interesting to compare my rereading of the myth of the Garden of Eden with the theory of eschatological history that is outlined in M. H. Abrams, *Natural Supernaturalism* (New York: W. W. Norton, 1971).

16. Jacques Lacan, *The Four Fundamental Concepts of Psychoanalysis*, translated by Alan Sheridan (New York: W. W. Norton, 1981), pp. 210–213.

17. I am indebted to the Thomas Cohen, who first taught me how to "read" Hitchcock's films.

18. A criticism of the attempt to equate women with the unrepresentable Real is a constant theme in both Judith Butler's

Bodies That Matter and Luce Irigaray's *The Sex Which Is Not One*.

19. Jacques Lacan, *The Four Fundamental Concepts of Psychoanalysis*, p. 209.

20. Lacan's phenomenological account of consciousness is best grasped in his chapter entitled "A Materialist Definition of the Phenomenon of Consciousness," in *The Seminar of Jacques Lacan, Book II: The Ego in Freud's Theory* edited by Jacques-Alain Miller and translated by Sylvana Tomaselli (New York: W. W. Norton, 1988), 40–52.

21. Judith Butler, *Bodies That Matter* (New York: Routledge, 1993), represents an extended attempt to use Lacan's theories of the real and the object (*a*) in order to analyze different processes of racial and sexual abjection.

22. This process of the projection of male loss onto female bodies is the central theme of Kaja Silverman, *The Acoustic Mirror*, pp. 1–41.

Chapter 1: *The Lady Vanishes*, but the Letter Remains

1. For an extended analysis of the Oedipal level of this film, see Raymond Durgnat, *The Strange Case of Alfred Hitchcock* (Cambridge: MIT Press, 1974).

2. For more on this theory, see Patrice Petro, "Rematerializing the Vanishing "Lady," in *The Hitchcock Reader*, edited by Marshall Deutelbaum and Leland Poague, (Ames: Iowa State Univ. Press, 1992), pp. 122–133.

3. I am indebted to Thomas Cohen for his articulation of this notion of materiality and for introducing me to a new way of reading Hitchcock.

4. For an in depth analysis of the masculine control of speech in film, see Kaja Silverman, *The Acoustic Mirror*, p. 24.

5. Jacques Lacan, "On the Possible Treatment of Psychosis," in *Ecrits: A Selection*, translated by Alan Sheridan, (New York: Norton, 1977), p. 200.

6. For a further discussion of the difference between metaphor and metonymy in Lacan's theory, see Jean-Luc Nancy

and Philippe Lecoue-Lebarthe, *The Title of the Letter: A Reading of Lacan*, Francois Raffoul and David Pettigrew, trs. (Albany: State University of New York Press, 1992).

7. Sigmund Freud, *The Interpretation of Dreams* (New York: Avon Books, 1985), p. 316.

8. Julia Kristeva, *Revolution in Poetic Language*, (New York: Columbia Univ. Press, 1980), p. 31.

9. See Petro's excellent discussion of this process on p. 126 of "Rematerializing the Vanishing "Lady"".

10. Julia Kristeva, *The Powers of Horror*, Leon Roudiez, tr. (New York: Columbia Univ. Press, 1982), p. 77.

11. Julia Kristeva, *Desire in Language*, Leon Roudiez, ed. (New York: Columbia Univ. Press, 1980), p. 23.

12. William Rothman was one of the first to point out this symbol of the bar in his book *Hitchcock—The Murderous Gaze* (Cambridge: Harvard Univ. Press, 1982).

13. Petro, "Rematerializing The Vanishing "Lady", p. 124.

14. For a further discussion of Lacan's rereading of Freud's theory of the death drive, see Samuels, *Between Philosophy and Psychoanalysis*, pp. 107–131.

15. Sigmund Freud, *Beyond The Pleasure Principle* (New York: W. W. Norton, 1959), p. 8.

16. Elisabeth Bronfen, "The Lady Vanishes: Sophie Freud and Beyond The Pleasure Principle," in *South Atlantic Quarterly*, 88 (Fall 1989), no. 4: 961–992.

Chapter 2: The Fear of Women and Writing in *Spellbound*

1. Silverman, *The Acoustic Mirror*.

2. For an explanation of Lacan's theory of discourse, see Samuels, *Between Philosophy and Psychoanalysis*, pp. 79–147, and Mark Bracher, *Lacan, Discourse, and Social Change* (Ithaca: Cornell Univ. Press, 1993).

3. Judith Butler returns to this criticism in her *Bodies That Matter*, p. 189.

4. The connection between discourse and power runs throughout Michel Foucault's work, especially in *Discipline and Punish* (New York: Vintage, 1979), and *Language, Counter-Memory, Practice* (Ithaca: Cornell Univ. Press, 1977).

5. See Judith Butler's excellent discussion of this process of exclusion in *Bodies that Matter*, pp. 187–222.

6. Kristeva, *Powers of Horror*, pp. 1–31.

7. I believe that I am indebted to Thomas Cohen for pointing out this connection between writing and black lines on a white surface.

8. Thomas Hyde, "The Moral Universe of Hitchcock's *Spellbound*," in *A Hitchcock Reader*, edited by Marshall Deutelbaum and Leland Poague (Ames: Iowa State Univ., 1986), p. 158.

9. Jacques Derrida, *On Grammatology* (Baltimore: Johns Hopkins Univ. Press, 1976).

10. Jacques Lacan, *The Four Fundamental Concepts of Psychoanalysis*, p. 26.

11. Sigmund Freud, *Group Psychology and the Analysis of the Ego* (New York: W. W. Norton, 1959), pp. 34–38.

12. This complex connection between identification, murder, and object-loss seems to be inherent to the feminine version of the Oedipus Complex. See Juliana Schiesari, *The Gendering of Melancholia* (Ithaca: Cornell Univ. Press, 1992), pp. 63–95.

13. Sigmund Freud, *Totem and Taboo* (New York: W. W. Norton, 1950), pp. 125–126, 141–142, 149.

14. For a further elaboration of this notion of repetition, see Lacan's *Four Fundamental Concepts of Psychoanalysis*, pp. 39–40.

15. Sigmund Freud, *Beyond the Pleasure Principle*, pp. 8–11.

16. See Sigmund Freud's early, "Project for a Scientific Psychology," in *The Origins of Psychoanalysis* (New York: Basic Books, 1954), and "A Note Upon the 'Mystic Writing Pad,'" in *General Psychological Theory* (New York: Collier Books, 1963) for this association between writing and memory.

17. Hyde, "The Moral Universe of Hitchcock's *Spellbound*," p. 155.

18. It would be strange if these four directors relate to the four levels of castration that we attached to John Ballantine's

pathology. Just as J. B. killed his brother in the real, Dr. Murchison murdered the real Dr. Edwardes. This murder was then covered up through the appearance of the fake Dr. Edwardes, who himself used this false identity to escape from his initial crime.

19. Both Thomas Hyde (153) and Slavoj Zizek in *Tout ce que Vous avez Toujours voulu savoir sur Lacan sans jamais oser le demander a Hitchcock* (Paris: Navarin, 1988), p. 89, argue that this film presents an unproblematic and conservative description of psychoanalysis. I am, of course, trying to show how Hitchcock's film shows an insightful understanding of some of the most important and neglected aspects of psychoanalysis.

20. One cannot help but read Hitchcock's interviews with Truffaut as a classic attempt at self-dissimulation.

21. Kaja Silverman, *Male Subjectivity at the Margins* (New York: Routledge, 1992), p. 54.

22. Luce Irigaray, *Speculum of the Other Woman* (Ithaca: Cornell Univ. Press, 1985), p. 71.

23. Modleski, *The Women Who Knew Too Much.*

24. This passage obviously refers to Judith Butler's work in *Gender Trouble* (New York: Routledge Press, 1990), and *Bodies That Matter.*

Chapter 3: *Rebecca*, Repetition, and the Circulation of Feminine Desire

1. In this opening monologue, Hitchcock and his scriptwriter transform and edit Daphne du Maurier's original text.

2. Silverman, *The Acoustic Mirror.*

3. For an extended discussion of the relationship between the death drive and masculinity, see Samuels, *Between Philosophy and Psychoanalysis*, chapter 6.

4. For a discussion of this relationship between the real and repetition in Hitchcock and Lacan, see Thomas Cohen, *Anti-Mimesis From Plato To Hitchcock* (New York: Cambridge Univ. Press, 1994), p. 63.

5. The paradoxical nature of Freud's theory of the object-choice receives its strongest articulation in Freud's three essays on "The Contributions to the Psychology of Love," in *On Sexuality*, edited and translated by James Struchey (New York: Penguin Books, 1977), pp. 227–284.

6. Butler, *Bodies That Matter*, pp. 187–222.

7. This notion of the circulation of feminine desire by women adds a new twist to Eve Sedgwick's analysis of homosocial desire.

8. This notion of lesbian homosocial desire is intended to be an extension of Eve Sedgwick's theory of male homosocial desire. Hitchcock's film helps to explore an aspect of our culture that is most often ignored by literary and film critics.

9. In fact, in Lacan's articulation of the schema R, he states that the Imaginary relation between the ego and its specular image serves as a "homologue for the Mother/Child Symbolic relation" (Lacan, 1977, 196).

10. Modleski, *The Women Who Knew Too Much* points out that the structure of the narrative in *Rebecca* does not follow the Oedipus Complex, but rather it is structured by the Electra Complex (46).

11. Freud, *Totem and Taboo*, pp. 75–78.

12. Lacan articulates his theory of the letter in many texts, but a first place to look for a theory of the materiality of language is in his *Ecrits* "The Agency of the Letter in the Unconscious," p. 146–178.

13. While the circulation of feminine desire may threaten masculine structures, it is clear that the display of lesbian sexuality is a central aspect of male-oriented pornography.

Chapter 4: *Notorious*

1. Modleski, *The Women Who Knew Too Much*, p. 60.

2. Lee Edelman, "Seeing Things: Representations, the Scene of Surveillance, and the Spectacle of Gay Male Sex," in *Inside/out*, edited by Diana Fuss (New York: Routledge, 1991), pp. 93–116.

3. Silverman, *Male Subjectivity at the Margins*.

4. Irigaray, *The Sex Which Is Not One*, pp. 106–107.

5. For an analysis of this Irigary's strategy see Butler, *Bodies that Matter*, pp. 35–38.

6. See Julia Kristeva's discussion of the feminine form and the structure of masculinity in her theory of abjection in *Powers of Horror*.

7. I believe that most feminist theories of alternative modes of discourse have concentrated on verbal and written language and have not seriously questioned how one can develop alternative modes of visual representation.

8. For an analysis of this diamond shape, see my chapter in this book on *Marnie*.

9. As an object of circulation, one is reminded here of Zizek's analysis of the object (a) in the symbolic structure of exchange. See Slavoj Zizek, *The Sublime Object of Ideology* (New York: Verso, 1989), p. 182.

10. By searching for the secret of her feminine nature, Alicia is investigating the foundations of her own sexuality and the mystery of birth, which Freud most often attaches to the male subject's quest for knowledge.

11. Lacan argues in his seminar on "The Purloined Letter" that whoever possess the letter loses all possibility of acting and is thus feminized.

Chapter 5: *Vertigo*

1. Slavoj Zizek, *Looking Awry*, p. 85.

2. Marian Keane, "A Closer Look at Scopophilia: Mulvey, Hitchcock, and *Vertigo*," in *The Hitchcock Reader*, p. 234.

3. Freud presents this dream in his *Interpretation of Dreams*, chapter 2, and Lacan gives an extended reading of it in his *The Seminar of Jacques Lacan: Book II The Ego in Freud's Theory and in the Technique of Psychoanalysis*, pp. 146–174.

4. For an extended discussion of this relationship between consciousness and the unity of the body, see chapter 2 of Samuels, *Between Philosophy and Psychoanalysis*, pp. 59–74.

5. Mary Anne Doane discusses this relationship between lack, the Real, and the feminine form in her *Femmes Fatales* (New York, Routledge, 1991), pp. 20–24.

6. Lee Edelman, "Seeing Things: Representation, the Scene of Surveillance, and the Spectacle of Gay Male Sex," in *inside / out* (New York: Routledge, 1991), p. 97.

7. See Lacan's discussion of the Moebious strip and other topological forms in *The Four Fundamental Concepts of Psychoanalysis*, pp. 22, 34, 74, 89–90, 131, 144, 147, 155–156, 161, 164, 181, 184, 203, 209.

8. Lacan, *The Seminar of Jacques Lacan: Book VII*, p. 71.

9. For a discussion of the schema L, see Jacques Lacan, *Ecrits: A Selection*, Alan Sheridan, tr. (New York: W. W. Norton, 1977), pp. 193–196.

10. Lacan, *The Ethics of . . .* , p. 68.

11. Lacan articulates the connection between the Imaginary and the sublimation of the object in his *Ethics Seminar*, p. 99.

12. Juliana Schiesari, *The Gendering of Melancholia* (New York: Cornell Univ. Press, 1992).

13. Karen Horney, *Feminine Psychology* (New York: W. W. Norton, 1973), p. 135.

14. Sigmund Freud, "On the Universal Tendency to Debasement in the Sphere of Love," in *On Sexuality* (New York: Penguin Books, 1977), pp. 247–260.

15. Zizek has an excellent discussion of the relationship between death and the love-object in his analysis of *Vertigo* in *Looking Awry*, pp. 83–87.

16. Lacan, *The Ethics of . . .* , p. 112.

17. Lacan's theory of Courtly Love follows Freud's analysis of the conditions of the love-object in his "Three Contributions to the Psychology of Love, *On Sexuality*, pp. 227–284.

18. Robin Wood discusses this connection between power, masculinity, and freedom in his essay entitled "Male Desire, Male Anxiety: The Essential Hitchcock," in *The Hitchcock Reader*, edited by Marshall Deutelbaum and Leland Poague, p. 226.

19. In his *Ethics* seminar, Lacan argues that the connection between the death drive and the signifier is due in part to the way

that language can create something out of nothing."Will to destruction. Will to make a fresh start. Will for an Other-thing, given that everything can be challenged from the perspective of the function of the signifier. If everything that is immanent or implicit in the chain of natural events may be considered as subject to the so-called death drive, it is only because there is a signifying chain" (212).

20. Lacan analyzes the three main ways that the subject relates to the void of the Thing in science, art, and religion, in his *Ethics* seminar, p. 130.

21. Sigmund Freud, "Mourning and Melancholia," in *General Psychological Theory*, edited by Philip Rieff (New York: Collier Books, 1963), pp. 164–179.

22. For Lacan's analysis of the look as a stain, see Lacan, *The Four Fundamental Concepts of Psychoanalysis*, pp. 96–102.

23. Freud connects the drive to the overcoming of pity and shame in his *Three Essays on The Theory of Sexuality*, James Strachey, ed. (New York: Basic Books, 1962), pp. 27–28.

24. This problematic concerning the different relationship that men and women have to language, death, and representation is the central theme of Juliana Schiesari, *The Gendering of Melancholia*.

Chapter 6: Marnie

1. For a discussion of this relationship between the Real and feminine writing, see this book chapters 1 and 2.

2. Butler's *Bodies That Matter*.

3. Piso, "Mark's Marnie," in *A Hitchcock Reader* (Ames: Iowa State U. Press, 1986), p. 298, points out this repetition of the "mar" but does not interpret it.

4. Zdenko Vrdlouec makes this same connection between the mother, murder, and the letter M in Slavoj Zizek's *Tout ce que Vous avez toujours voulu savoir sur Lacan sans jamais oser le demander a Hitchcock*, p. 21.

5. Kristeva, *Powers of Horror*.

6. See Samuels discussion of the hysterical symptom in *Between Philosophy and Psychoanalysis*, pp. 45, 53–54, 76–77, 85–89.

7. See Piso, "Mark's Marnie," and Ian Cameron and Richard Jeffery, "The Universal Hitchcock," in *The Hitchcock Reader*, pp. 270–277.

8. Lacan articulates this relation between the mirror stage and the identification with the symbolic name in his texts on "The Mirror Stage" and "Aggressivity in Psychoanalysis," in *Ecrits: A Selection*, p. 1–29.

9. Butler, *Bodies That Matter*, p. 93–119. We must keep in mind that Marnie does not construct her identity out of nothing, rather she steals her signifiers from the Other. This supports Butler's claim that even constructed forms of identity are constrained and related to the symbolic Other.

10. One could question here if this separation of language from the realm of extra-textual referentiality is something that is inherently empowering and which men in our culture have continuously used to enhance their privileged positions.

11. Slavoj Zizek's analysis of the external materiality of ideology is of significance here. See Zizek, *The Sublime Object of Ideology*, pp. 34–40.

12. Tania Modleski makes this same claim of bisexual identifications in Hitchcock's works throughout her *The Women Who Knew Too Much*.

13. For a further articulation of this split between the gaze and the viewpoint, see Lacan's *Four Fundamental Concepts of Psychoanalysis*, pp. 67–119.

14. For this connection between "Alfred" and "Albert" see Thomas Cohen, *Anti-Mimesis From Plato To Hitchcock*, p. 241.

15. I do not want to imply here that critical interpretations should replace political transformations. Rather, I would like to argue that certain forms of critical analysis can have real political effects.

16. Julia Kristeva, "Identification and the Real" in *Literary Theory Today*, edited by Peter Collier and Helga Geyer-Ryan (Ithaca: Cornell Univ. Press, 1990), pp. 167–176.

17. Sigmund Freud, "Female Sexuality" in *On Sexuality* (New York: Penguin Books, 1977), p. 371.

18. For Freud the vagina stays a mystery for both sexes until the time of puberty. At this point, its discovery is connected to the

Symbolic scene of castration and the general socialization of the subject's desire.

19. See Freud's discussion of this process in his *Three Essays on The Theory of Sexuality*, p. 87.

20. This theory of self-abjection is crucial to any psychoanalytic understanding of gay and lesbian subjectivities.

Chapter 7: Rear Window Ethics

1. Laura Mulvey, "Visual Pleasure and Narrative Cinema," in *Issues in Feminist Film Criticism*, Patricia Erens, ed. (Bloomington: Indiana Univ. Press, 1990), pp. 28–40.

2. Lacan, *The Four Fundamental Concepts of Psychoanalysis*.

3. The translators often use both "look" and "gaze" in order to translate the French word "regard."

4. See Jean Paul Satre, *Being and Nothingness* (New York: Washington Square Press, 1977), Section 3 for a more extended elaboration of this notion of the gaze. In Lacan's *Four Fundamental Concepts of Psychoanalysis*, p. 84, he both repeats and challenges Sartre's interpretation of this phenomenon.

5. For a further exploration of this opposition between the gaze and vision, see Samuels, *Between Philosophy and Psychoanalysis*, pp. 59–74.

6. Modleski, *The Women Who Knew Too Much*, p. 77, accurately highlights Lisa's activity and Jefferies inactivity.

7. Zizek, *Looking Awry*, p. 92.

8. Edelman, "Seeing Things: Representation," pp. 93–118.

9. Eve Sedgwick, *Between Men: English Literature*.

10. Modleski, *The Women Who Knew Too Much*, p. 77, makes this argument. She also quotes Hitchcock's own acknowledgement of these parallel identifications.

11. An excellent analysis of the differences between the denotation and connotation of homosexuality in Hitchcock's film, can be found in D. A. Miller, "Anal Rope," in Inside/Out, pp. 119–141.

12. Throughout this essay, I have been using the term "masculine" to denote a performative state of sexual activity, and the term "feminine" to relate to a performance of passivity. At the same time, I am also trying to point to the failures of this Freudian binary that does not take into account diverse forms of identification and sexual desire.

Chapter 8: The Birds

1. Margaret Horowitz, "*The Birds*: A Mother's Love," in *The Hitchcock Reader*, edited by Marshall Deutelbaum and Leland Poague (Ames: Iowa State Univ. Press, 1986), pp. 279–288.

2. Zizek, *Looking Awry*.

3. Robin Wood, *Hitchcock's Films* (New York: A. S. Barnes and Company, 1977), p. 116.

4. For an extended analysis of the anti-mimetic and anti-communicative foundations of language, see Tom Cohen, *Anti-Mimesis From Plato To Hitchcock* (New York: Cambridge Univ. Press, 1994).

5. For an extended discussion of the relation between consciousness and nothingness, see Samuels, *Between Philosophy and Psychoanalysis*, pp. 59–74.

6. The proliferation of different ideological explanations of the birds in the film itself, shows Hitchcock's awareness of the different ways that his own films can and will be read. This also means that the very acts of reading and interpretation are inscribed and challenged within the very text of the film.

7. My strategy in this discussion is to combine a radical critique of the processes of representation with an account of the way that meaning and ideology is produced on an imaginary level.

8. Modleski, *The Women Who Knew Too Much*, p. 2.

9. We must remember that Lacan writes the structure of the fundamental fantasy in the discourse of analysis as: $a \dashrightarrow \$$ (the object causes the desire and splitting of the subject). This structure represents a reversal of the imaginary fantasy ($\$\hat{v}a$) that one finds at the bottom of the discourse of the master. This could mean that analysis entails a reversal of linguistic mastery and a crossing through or reversal of the imaginary fantasy.

10. Zizek, *Sublime Object*, p. 3.

11. Zizek, *Looking Awry*, p. 6.

Epilogue

1. Freud, *Three Essays on the Theory of Sexuality*, pp. 56–57, n.1.

2. My use of the Lacanian notion of the "Real," here, attempts to relate together the reality of perception with the limits of all forms of Symbolization.

3. For a detailed analysis of the relationship between the Real and psychosis, see Samuels, *Between Philosophy and Psychoanalysis*, pp. 27–55.

4. Sigmund Freud, "On Narcissism: An Introduction," edited by Philip Rieff in *General Psychological Theory* (New York: Collier Books, 1963), p. 75.

5. Barbara Klinger, "*Psycho*: The Institutionalization of Female Sexuality," in *The Hitchcock Reader*, edited by Marshall Deutelbaum and Leland Poague (Ames: Iowa State Univ., 1986), p. 334.

6. For an extended analysis of the meaning of these "mar" names, see my chapter in this book on *Marnie*.

7. This same relation between money, language, and a pound of flesh is of course a central theme to Shakespeare's *Merchant of Venice*.

8. Zizek, *Looking Awry*.

9. Norman's horror of blood connects him to Marnie and the general connection between femininity, abjection, and male anxiety.

Index

163